A DAY OF FREEDOM

"It is for freedom that Christ has set us free . . ."

Galatians 5:1

by Robert E. and Charlyne A. Steinkamp

A DAY OF FREEDOM

by Robert and Charlyne Steinkamp

ISBN 1-892230-09-7

Rejoice Ministries, Inc.
Post Office Box 11242
Pompano Beach, Florida 33060
(954) 941-6508
www.rejoiceministries.org

All scripture quotations in this book are from the
HOLY BIBLE, NEW INTERNATIONAL VERSION.
Copyright 1973, 1978, 1984 International Bible Society.
Used by permission

Printed in the United States of America

IN APPRECIATION

Although only two names appear on the cover of this book, we are deeply indebted to many others. They made it possible for us to take the thoughts that the Lord had given us, and to share them with you in printed form.

Julie Bell and Dennis Wingfield, board members of Rejoice Ministries, Inc. assisted in the publication of this book, as both have done with other Rejoice books. Kimberly Kuebler, the ministry's Administrative Assistant, carried out a vital role in manuscript preparation.

The Lord was so good to us in providing for final editing. Before the manuscript was completed, He sent a college professor, a published author himself, into our lives. Dr. Conley K. McMullen is also standing for the restoration of his own marriage. Conley's professional skills, combined with his sweet spirit and conviction about the covenant of marriage, could be sensed in his corrections and suggestions.

We are also indebted to friends who read the manuscript, prayed for us, and helped provide for printing expenses. May the Lord God whom made *A Day of Freedom* possible bless each one who helped.

DEDICATION

This book is dedicated to men and women around the world who have refused to surrender their families to satan. They have chosen to stand a stand, praying for a return of their prodigal spouse, first to the Lord God, and then to a loving and waiting family.

May each of these dedicated people find something on these pages that will encourage them to fight the spiritual battle for the eternal destiny of their mate's soul.

Bob and Charlyne Steinkamp

A DAY OF FREEDOM

TABLE OF CONTENTS

Many Are The Plans In A Man's Heart,
But It Is The Lord's Purpose That Prevails.
Proverbs 19:21

INTRODUCTION

Chapter 1 1
Chapter 2 9
Chapter 3 11
Chapter 4 20
Chapter 5 27
Chapter 6 31
Chapter 7 44
Chapter 8 54
Chapter 9 64
Chapter 10 73
Chapter 11 78
Chapter 12 82
Chapter 13 89
Chapter 14 93
Chapter 15 97
Chapter 16 101
There Is Freedom In Christ 110
Join God's Army 114
Who Is The Enemy? 121
Weapons Of Our Warfare 131
The Lord Can Deliver 143
Other Scriptures 146
Standing and Praying 154

Introducing Rejoice Ministries
Do You Really Want A Divorce?
Additional Materials Available
The Greatest News

INTRODUCTION

My wife and I are indeed blessed. We both know the Lord. He restored our marriage in 1987, two years after we were divorced. Since that time, God has allowed us to minister His hope and love to hurting spouses through Rejoice Marriage Ministries.

This book, our tenth, is a combination of both of our writing styles. God has given me several fiction stories that demonstrate the covenant of marriage. Charlyne has an anointed way of teaching the Bible through her writing.

A Day of Freedom started out to be a 96 page fiction story. As the story developed, it became clear to both of us that Charlyne needed to write a chapter at the end of the book. Under the guidance of the Holy Spirit, her "chapter" expanded to 50 pages.

In my section, you will read about man's problems. Charlyne then shares God's provisions. We pray that your walk with Christ toward a healed marriage might be strengthened by this book, which starts out all fiction, and concludes all fact.

May God bless you,
Bob (and Charlyne)

A DAY OF FREEDOM

CHAPTER 1

Delores Taylor stared intently into the flames in front of her, almost as though the solution to all of her problems could be found there. Suddenly, with a loud POP, the flames extinguished themselves. Sobbing, Dee dropped into the lawn chair next to her.

"It's no use," she whimpered, "Things will never be the same. I just can't do it. Everyone is right. I need to get on with my life. God must have a husband to do stuff like this for me." Looking at the challenge of six half-cooked hamburgers lying there, Dee composed herself and made another attempt to light the Taylor's old, rusting grill.

"Lord," she prayed aloud, "I call on You for big stuff, but now I need Your help to get ready for a July 4th picnic with my family. Please God, help me light my grill. Amen." Dee had already forgotten her prayer a minute later when she struck a match and an even, orange flame filled the backyard grill for the first time that afternoon.

Band music drifted from the portable radio sitting next to her chair; *America, America, God shed His grace on thee . . .* Listening to the music, combined with the sizzle of cooking meat under the bright Kentucky sunshine, seemed to boost Dee's spirits. With no one in sight, she soon found herself leading an imaginary band with the spatula she held in her hand. As quickly as she had started, the spatula dropped to her side and a frown returned to Dee's face. Rapidly changing emotions were not new to Dee these days.

"God's grace? Where is it? Maybe shed on America, but certainly not shed on our family. Where did I go wrong?" Turning her face heavenward, Dee asked aloud, "God, please show me where I went wrong." Dee again sat down in her folding chair, almost as if expecting the Lord to reply to her right then. Perhaps she just wasn't ready to hear from on high.

Dee and Tony had been married for eighteen years. They had met at church even before there was a ministry for singles. Their attraction to each other was almost immediate, and they married six months later. Their son, John, was now sixteen. Ten years earlier, they had adopted Deborah when she was an infant.

Until a year before, Tony had done an excellent job as spiritual leader of the Taylor family. All four of the Taylors had a personal relationship with the Lord. Each Sunday they could be found in church, where both Tony and Dee sang in the choir. In fact, music was the second love of the family. Tony would fill in when their worship leader was away. Dee could play both piano and organ. John had played drums since he was a young child. Deborah sang in the children's choir at church and had just started piano lessons when the Taylor problems began. Due to financial problems, those lessons had to be stopped, despite Deborah's objections.

"Mommy, everybody knows music but me," Deborah had shrieked through her tears. "It's not my fault if you guys are jerks and want to get divorced!"

"No one wants to get divorced," Dee had fired back. "There are some things that just happen and can't be helped."

"Do something, Mommy. Just do something to bring Daddy home," she had pleaded. "Ask God to do something to make it all go away and for us to be happy again."

"There are some things," Dee replied with a certain resolve in her voice, "that even God can't fix, and I'm afraid the mess our family is in is one of those things."

If you had been asked to select a family from their church that might become a victim of divorce, the Taylors would be one of the last to be considered. They looked like the model Christian family. Yet, that is exactly why they had come under the enemy's attack.

Satan does not fear the family that is already living for him. It is the family who has the ability to accomplish much for the cause of Christ that satan will single out.

Listening to the mix of patriotic music and sizzling hamburgers, Dee thought back to what had happened to the Taylor family. Although Tony had moved out of their home several months before, he and his wife continued to talk by phone from time to time. The calls usually started out to be about the children, but on occasion turned to their hopeless marriage.

During one such call, Tony confessed to his wife what had happened. He was a mechanic at an automobile dealership in downtown Paducah. Tony had worked for the same firm since before they were married. He had always been open about his faith in Jesus Christ. Tony had picked up the nickname "Preacher Man" years before, because he would often sit alone at lunch, eating, and reading his Bible.

It was something of a joke in the shop that when they had a car problem that could not be identified, Preacher Man would be called over. None of the other mechanics knew how often Tony would silently ask the Lord for guidance, that He might be praised when the problem was located. "Give the Lord the credit. He helps me solve my problems," was Tony's usual reply.

One day at noon, Tony went to the lockers to pick up his lunch and Bible and discovered that someone had hung a calendar on his locker door. It was the variety of calendar that the tool companies often gave away. The photo was of a female who was barely dressed.

"Hey, Preacher Man," someone called out from among the laughter, "anyone look like that over at the church?" Tony saw that most of his co-workers were in on the joke and were awaiting his response.

"That's not even funny," was the only comment Tony could utter. He quickly grabbed the calendar and stuck it inside his locker, in an attempt to get it out of sight as soon as possible. He reached for his lunch and Bible and went to an isolated area of the break room to eat. He became aware of the continued laughter of his co-workers as he sat down.

Tony unpacked his sandwich and opened his Bible, but did not read many verses that day. He thought about what had just happened. He also thought about the image that was now in his locker. Even through his embarrassment, there was a tingle deep inside Tony over what he had viewed.

Tony forgot the incident until quitting time that day. He opened his locker and suddenly saw that image. With no one watching, he stared for several seconds. Tony's thoughts raced here and there, even after he had closed the locker door. Feeling ashamed, he secured the lock, leaving the calendar lying on top of his Bible.

That evening, Tony recalled every detail of that image several times. Each such incident was accompanied by that same tingle that he had experienced at noon. Each such incident was also followed by incredible guilt. The process must have been exhausting, because Tony was just "too wiped out" to have devotions with his family that evening.

The next morning, Tony anxiously opened his locker knowing what awaited him . His co-workers soon forgot the incident, but Tony was still receiving a tingle each time he opened the door to his locker.

That following Sunday, Tony told Dee that he had a "tickle" in his throat and could not sing in the choir that day. In truth, he was embarrassed over what had been happening that week. Tony's tickle was not in his throat.

Then came the day Tony opened his locker and felt nothing. No, he was not over the incident. He wanted to see more. That afternoon, Tony took a different route home, stopping at a small rural convenience store on the way. Feeling ashamed, he walked to the counter, pointed to a magazine in a rack behind it, and mumbled "One of those," without ever making eye contact with the clerk.

Back behind the wheel of his car, Tony removed the plastic wrapper and browsed through the magazine. The tingle that he had sensed in front of his locker had returned, only this time stronger. The enemy had exposed Tony Taylor to an addiction and he had not resisted. As with any addiction, it was going to take more and more to keep Tony "tingling." The cost of his addiction would be his family, his self-respect, and even his marriage.

Before reaching home, Tony had returned that magazine to its plastic cover and had hidden it behind the spare tire in his automobile. Many times that evening he thought about what he had hidden away. He even wished that Dee would leave on an errand so that he could read the articles in his magazine.

That next day, he began to eat lunch in his car. Each Sunday, Tony could be found all shined up in church with his family. Each weekday at noon, he could be found reading filth in his car, but no one knew. He would munch on a sandwich and thumb through page after page of filth. Then came the day that he discovered a love note from Dee tucked into his lunch. Tony's guilt was erased for the moment when he opened his magazine. His loving wife and her sweet words were quickly forgotten.

There came a day when Tony threw away his magazine. No, he had not obeyed the conviction of God to do so. Those images and words no longer gave him the addictive thrills that he sought. That day, on the way home, Tony stopped at that same convenience store and purchased two magazines. He could barely wait for the next day.

Tony's life soon began to change drastically. He started to withdraw from his family and from the church he had loved so much. But the most dramatic change was that he had withdrawn from the God that he loved even more.

"It must not be too bad," Tony attempted to reason with himself one day, "because no one preaches about stuff like that anymore. With the Internet and all, I guess times have changed and everyone just accepts it. Besides, what does it hurt? It's not like it is another person or anything."

In rapid succession, Tony's addiction for pornography had moved him from magazines to videos. The same VCR that filled the Taylor home with praise music one day, would be filling it with unimaginable audio and video when Tony was home alone. It was not long before the videos did not satisfy Tony. He visited an "adult entertainment" den of sin across the river from Paducah in Illinois.

"What does it hurt?" Tony would reason with himself over and over. "It's not like I'm having an affair with a woman I want to leave home for. I guess most men must do these things once in a while, because no one ever talks about it being wrong."

Tony's reasoning about "once in a while" was not valid, because most men do not do "these things" at all. Yes, most men might have a temptation to do "these things," but the wise man can follow the Biblical instruction given us in II Corinthians, chapter 10, verse 5: *We demolish arguments and every pretension that sets itself up against the knowledge of God, and we take captive every thought to make it obedient to*

Christ.

Tony's addiction to pornography only increased as time went on. Soon, one trip a week would not satisfy Tony, and he went across the Ohio River more often. He began to collect telephone numbers from some of the females that he met in those places. Tony had to lie to Dee so that he would have the money and the time for these encounters. In order for her to believe these lies, Tony had to build lie upon lie.

His church attendance and involvement had stopped completely. Tony refused to worship with "hypocrites," and blew out of proportion every imagined wrong at the church he once loved.

Didn't a Christian man caught up in something like this feel guilty? Yes, Tony, much like anyone involved in pornography, was filled with guilt. The rush that Tony experienced each time he passed that **WELCOME TO ILLINOIS** sign on the bridge was replaced by even greater guilt when he passed **YOU ARE NOW ENTERING KENTUCKY** on the return trip.

Within 24 hours, Tony would have forgotten that guilt, and looked forward to seeing the Illinois sign once again. Even though the guilt would have lessened, the shame that Brother Taylor experienced was building layer upon layer in his once-soft heart. The results were relationships with his Lord, his wife, his children, and his friends that continued to fall apart.

"Wasn't God speaking to one of His disobedient children?" you might be asking. Yes, the Lord was speaking in a thousand and one ways, but Tony was not listening. The Lord had yet to get his attention. Tony suspected that one television preacher must know his story, after overhearing comments against pornography on a program that Dee was watching.

"Brother, that stuff will draw every bit of life from you, if you don't repent and seek God's forgiveness and help to break the enemy's destructive cycle. It is bad, but God is good. He wants to clean and help you, right now!" Tony had to leave the room, fearing the tears welling up in his eyes would give away his secret sin to Dee.

Tony could have stayed if he had been aware of what the Lord had already revealed to his wife, Dee. Several weeks before, she had sensed, as only a one-flesh mate can do, that something was very wrong in their marriage. She had asked the Lord to reveal to her any changes in her life that she needed to make. Dee had been fasting every Friday for her marriage. She had intensified her spiritual warfare for her family. Each morning she was up an hour before Tony or her children, praying the armor of God on them. Despite her efforts, Tony only seemed to be lashing out at her, and at God even more. It was breaking her heart and she knew nothing else to do.

CHAPTER 2

Dee's prayer partner was Frances, an elderly widow in her church. Although years apart in age, they had become the closest of friends down through the years. Each time Dee would visit the small cottage where Frances lived, the concern would be shared and Frances would say, "Honey, let's talk to God about it." It seemed that God always answered Frances' prayers.

Not once had Dee heard anything she had shared with Frances repeated by a third person. Many times, though, Frances would call Dee on the phone and share a verse of scripture the Lord had given her. This was especially touching because Frances had lost most of her eyesight. Dee knew that each verse had been read one letter at a time through a huge magnifying glass. Dee also knew that her need was being carried to God by one of His precious and faithful saints.

One Saturday afternoon, two weeks before the television incident, while Tony was out with some new "friends" that he had met across the river in Illinois, Dee visited Frances and shared her concerns. Frances sat quietly, not saying a word, until Dee had poured out her heart and her fear that their marriage was falling apart.

"Honey, let's talk to God about it."

While they were praying, the Lord gave Frances a word of knowledge for Dee. Frances silently asked the Holy Spirit how He would have her share it.

"Dee, honey, could your Tony have sin in his life? The Holy Spirit, as best I can hear Him, seems to be saying that there is uncleanliness in Tony's life that He will bring out."

"What is it?"

"I don't know, and that really is not important. What is important is that you and I stand firm, praying for Tony to repent. Remember, this is not about your marriage. This is about Tony's eternal destiny. You and I do not want him to meet the Lord with unconfessed sin in his life."

Dee began to pray specifically that the Lord would bring out the uncleanliness in her husband's life. She prayed this way not so that she would know what sin was there, but so that the Lord could remove it and forgive Tony.

After Dee began to pray for Tony's uncleanliness to be brought out, he became more and more withdrawn and irritable with his family. Dee thought that the Lord was not hearing her prayers. She could not see the angels on the other side of her mountain chipping away at the circumstances. Part of that process was Tony's secret sin being revealed.

CHAPTER 3

One Saturday at the end of November, Tony was working around the outside of the Taylor home, preparing it for the approaching Kentucky winter. Dee sensed that she should ask her husband to go to church with his family the next day, for the first time in months. She went outdoors and stood next to the ladder where Tony was putting up storm windows.

"Honey, what do you have planned for tomorrow?" Dee cautiously asked.

"The usual."

"I was wondering, since this is Advent, if you would like to go to church with us this week."

"Advent," Tony thought, "nothing about Christmas is going to hurt. Besides, it will get her off my back for a while."

"Sure, I'll go," came Tony's surprising reply.

The next morning was like Sundays from months before. The Taylors were all going to church together. Once there, several of their friends greeted Tony warmly. Frances found her way across the narthex from the missionary table she had staffed faithfully for years to greet the man for whom she was praying so faithfully.

"Dear," she began, " it sure is good to see you in the Lord's house today. I pray for you every day." The hug she gave Tony brought back memories of his own grandmother hugging him and filled him with warmth. The collection of filth that he had carefully locked away in his gun locker on the floor of the Taylor's bedroom closet seemed a million miles away. That distance was about to shorten quickly that morning as an Advent sermon was being preached.

Tony was thankful that their senior pastor was out of town. Tony had been dodging his phone calls and notes for several months. Reverend Scott Wilson, a new associate pastor occupied the pulpit that morning. There was something about his way that Tony liked. Pastor Wilson preached as though he were talking to a friend. Tony liked his way until the new Pastor reached the focus of his sermon.

Pastor Wilson told about the origin of Advent. He then explained that Advent was a time of preparation of the heart for the coming of Christ. When he illustrated by saying that Advent is the time of the year when we should oil the hinges on the door to our heart, Tony's thoughts raced to the squeaking hinges on the seldom-used gun locker that hid his secret sin from the eyes of man, but not from God. He was just about to be reminded of that locker even more directly.

"Preparation demands that we take a careful look at our heart," the pastor preached. "We must cleanse any area that does not honor our Lord Jesus Christ. Something has crept into society that is destroying families. It is introduced in such a subtle way that we cannot even define it. It can start with a television program that goes too far. The advertisers use it to sell their products. Our children don't know where decency starts. We hear screams from the world about First Amendments rights..."

"No," Tony thought, "he wouldn't be going there. Man, this is Christmas!"

"This Advent Season is the time for Christians to rethink the line. Pornography is that evil. We have people sitting in my hearing today that have an addiction to pornography. That addiction will only increase until it destroys everything that is precious to you. Tossing the stuff that you have hidden is the beginning, but it is not the end. Only Jesus Christ can free you from those filthy chains that are forever tightening around you. Won't you allow the Lord to break those chains today?"

Tony could feel the blood draining from his face. His ears burned hot. He hoped that whoever was sitting behind him did not notice. "Who told this guy? This is ridiculous! It's almost Christmas and that is the best he can do? No wonder I don't come here very often."

From across that sanctuary, a little saint, holding a magnifying glass, looked at the Taylors. She saw Tony sitting perfectly still. Suddenly she knew. No other human would ever hear what the Lord had just revealed to her.

Frances bowed her head and prayed, "Thank You, Lord, for revealing to me exactly how I need to pray for Tony and Dee. God, You are so good. Please, Lord, clean out Tony's life and bring him back to You, Amen."

At the end of that service, Pastor Wilson drew the net. He invited people to receive Jesus Christ as Lord and Savior of their life, receiving His gift of eternal life. In addition, the Pastor also invited people to repent for their involvement with pornography, turning away from anything that they had been involved in, drawing a new line of decency around themselves and their families.

As best he could, Tony did serious business with God that day standing in his pew. Tony promised to dispose of everything that very day. He also promised the Lord that he would make no more trips across the river. Tony left that service feeling cleaner than he had in many months. It was almost as though he had not been away from church, and from the Lord, at all.

During the drive home, Dee commented about what they had just heard. She had no idea that her husband was involved in pornography, nor that he had silently called on the Lord for help. If Tony had any thought of confessing that sin to Dee, it was quickly erased.

"That was quite a sermon today, huh?" Dee inquired.

"Uh huh."

"I am so thankful the demon of pornography has stayed away from our home. I don't know how I could live with a husband who was viewing that filth, knowing that I was always being compared to someone or something he saw in a picture. Tony, I think we need to take a closer look at the television programs we allow into our home," Dee added. "We don't want to open the door even a small bit for the enemy." She had no idea that she was hitting her husband right between the eyes, just as the Lord had been doing for the past 45 minutes.

"Uh huh."

Tony's thoughts were on the contents of that gun box, not on his driving. He did not know how to break the bondage of pornography that had him bound. Yes, he would do as he had just promised the Lord and destroy his collection, but how would he stay away in the future from something that made him feel so good? He still did not know what a few magazines and videos that he viewed privately could hurt. In his mind, Tony was not associating his trips across the river and his repeated unfaithfulness with pornography.

Tony's attention was called back to his driving by the tap of a horn. He looked into the rear view mirror and saw the blue lights of a Kentucky State Trooper. As soon as he pulled over, Tony saw the largest, sternest looking law enforcement officer that he had ever seen.

"Good afternoon, sir. Driver's license, registration, and insurance card please."

Tony's tough mechanic's hands trembled as he attempted to locate the three requested documents in his wallet. "What did I do wrong, sir?" Tony responded with a quiver in his voice.

"Driver's license, registration, and insurance card please," the trooper repeated.

Credit cards dropped to the floor of the car, as Tony passed the three requested items out of his car window, one at a time.

In the back seat, John and Deborah quietly giggled and exchanged light jabs. Deborah leaned over and whispered to her brother, "Now Daddy knows how we feel when he yells at us for doing something wrong."

Tony's correction of his children had become harsher and more frequent during recent months. The man who previously could have been the model for correction by a Christian parent, had started lashing out at every real or imagined wrong by his children. He was especially hard on John, who had just started driving. Right then, John was especially enjoying watching the trooper make his dad squirm.

"How fast was I going, sir?"

"I clocked you at 48 miles an hour. This is a residential zone and the speed limit is 35."

"Um, sir, may I talk to you privately," Tony inquired. He glanced at the aluminum citation book in the trooper's hand, glistening under the noon day sun.

"Sir, stay in your car."

The trooper returned to his car and began to talk on the radio. Tony used the opportunity to lash out at his family.

"If I get a ticket, it is the fault of all three of you. Dee, you jabber so much that I can't even pay attention to my driving. From now on, shut up! I don't want to hear a thing from the back seat anytime this car is moving. Understood?"

"Yes sir," came two voices in unison from behind him.

In about two minutes, the trooper exited from his patrol car and motioned for Tony to join him between the two cars. Tony had seen on television that is what is done when a policeman is about to arrest someone. "What have I done?" he asked himself while getting out of the car.

Some might say that Tony had a guilty conscience. In truth, he was actually living every day under Holy Spirit conviction. Ever since he purchased his first pornographic magazine, Tony had been under the conviction of the Spirit of God to repent, to confess and turn away from his sin. That conviction had made him feel guilty about everything that he was doing. Our Lord God seeks His lost sheep, and He was not going to give up on Tony, regardless of the circumstances.

When Tony had first heard that horn and observed the blue lights, he could not stop his car fast enough. Now that the trooper was beckoning him out of the car, he could not get out fast enough. Why? Because that officer had the authority of the State of Kentucky behind him. Tony had to obey that authority.

The demon of pornography had entered Tony's life. He had never been taught that, as a child of God, he had the authority to pull over the pornography that had enslaved him. That trooper had not fought with Tony to get him out of the car. It only took an index finger beckoning for him to come.

As Christians, we need to realize the authority that our Heavenly Father has given His children to call out the demons that attempt to bind and destroy us. The trooper did not pull and tug to get Tony out of the car. He called him out. With heavenly authority behind us, we can call out anything the enemy has sent to bind us.

"Oh, but I have seen police officers fighting to subdue

people," you might be thinking. True, but the good guys always win. The police officer might have to pull out his spray to subdue an especially violent prisoner. You might have to pull out and use fasting on the demon that is attempting to destroy your family, but in heavenly work, as in police work, the good guys always win!

"Mr. Taylor, your driving record indicates that you haven't had a moving violation in the past ten years," the trooper began. Tony was relieved to notice that the ticket book had disappeared. "I am going to give you a verbal warning this time. This traffic stop has been flagged on your license and the next time you are stopped by a police officer you will be cited. Do you realize how much a ticket for 13 miles over the limit would have cost you today? Slow it down, sir."

"Than-thank you. I appreciate the break. I'll watch my speed."

"Now what did you want to tell me?" asked the trooper.

Since there was no ticket to talk his way out of, Tony suddenly felt foolish, but he continued. "My wife and I are having trouble. We are about to get divorced and I had a lot on my mind. That's why I was speeding," Tony explained.

The word "divorce" had never been mentioned by either Tony or Dee. There were two occasions when Tony thought about divorce. Going across the river, he thought about how much fun he could have if he were on his own, away from Dee. Coming back, filled with shame, he always thought they should get divorced because he did not deserve the love of a good wife and godly woman like Dee.

The trooper said nothing. His sunglasses did not allow Tony to see where he was staring. He noticed the officer's name tag. It read TREMONTE. After a silence that was most uncomfortable for Tony, Officer Tremonte spoke.

"It appears that your family is coming from church."

"Yessir. We go to Christian Life Fellowship."

Tony did not know where this guy was headed, but he awkwardly related their music ability, the activities the kids were in, and how much he and his wife loved that church. He neglected to mention this was the first Sunday that he had been in church for many weeks. It appeared to Tony that the trooper had suddenly shrunk about a foot in height and had lost all of his stern expression.

"Then why are you talking about tearing up your family by divorce?"

Tony wished the guy would have given him a citation instead of conversation. How would he answer this man's questions? "There is a lot of stuff in our marriage that won't go away," he blurted out. Tony failed to mention that he was the one who had introduced the "stuff" into their marriage.

"Mr. Taylor, alongside the road isn't the place to relate our story, but my wife and I went through some serious stuff years ago and the Lord God healed our marriage. If He can do that for me, I know that He can clean up and heal whatever is going on in your home."

"A man in Florida wrote a story about our marriage being healed. It is titled 'The Greatest Lover'. If you ever want to read it, call the post and ask to be connected to my voice mail. I would be glad to send you a copy."

"Greatest Lover? Is that you?"

"No sir, not quite," Trooper Tremonte replied. "That's all I am saying. Have a nice day, and watch your speed."

"What was that all about?" Dee asked as Tony got back

behind the wheel.

"Just talked my way out of a ticket," Tony answered. "That guy was a push over. Let's all go out to lunch on some of the money that I just saved us."

CHAPTER 4

Tony and Dee Taylor had long made it their practice to make Sunday a day of rest. It was seldom they went shopping on the Lord's Day. Nevertheless, Tony suggested on that day that Dee take Deborah and go Christmas shopping. Once again, he cited how much extra money he had, "...because I talked my way out of that ticket."

Although it was out of character for Tony to suggest that Dee go shopping, she readily agreed. Deborah was excited at the thought of having her mother's undivided attention for the afternoon.

Tony offered his son, John, the use of his car for the afternoon. This was really out of the ordinary. Naturally, his sixteen year old son jumped at the opportunity, but he did wonder what was up with his dad.

Recently, his requests to borrow the older car that Tony drove to work resulted in cross words, and usually denial of the request.

"Dad, what's wrong?" John had pleaded on one occasion. "You have ridden with me and told me what a good driver I am. Mrs. Humphries, from next door, told Mom how I let her out into traffic at the mall. Dad, let me grow up!"

It wasn't that Tony did not want John to grow up. Well, perhaps just a bit of that. Any dad becomes frightened as he watches his son grow into a man, knowing that some day that little boy, who grew up too fast, will leave home. Tony's repeated denials of John's requests to use a car, which would sit all weekend, were due to the secret sin that Tony had concealed behind the spare tire. Now that his books and magazines were secured in the gun box in his closet, he could be a dad once again.

There was another reason Tony had problems handing over to his son the keys to a nine year old car that otherwise would sit unused until he went to work Monday morning. From somewhere deep within, he recalled how he had used his family's car when he was just about John's age.

Tony could recall only some of the mischief that he and his buddy, Calvin, had gotten into. He remembered the lies that he had told his parents in order to facilitate the plans that he and Calvin had made for a meeting with a couple teen-age girls. There was one thing that Tony had forgotten about his teen years. He had forgotten about the magazine that he and Calvin had purchased and hidden under the rubber mat behind the spare tire.

By the standards of today's world, that magazine would be considered acceptable. In fact, we have gone so far that the photos from that magazine could be shown on late-night television today and no one would even notice. Nevertheless, Tony had set a stronghold into place twenty five years before that was about to destroy his marriage.

On that Sunday afternoon, with all of his family gone, it appeared that Tony was about to take the first step toward breaking the stronghold of pornography that had enslaved him. Holding in his hand the only existing key to the gun box, he stood in their bedroom, in front of the closet door, and wondered how to dispose of his collection of filth.

Just as he had done many times before when home alone, Tony knelt down and unlocked the box in the far end of the closet. The old hinges creaked as he opened the metal door. For the very first time, the photo on the cover of the magazine on top disgusted him. Tony felt his stomach tumble as he dropped the magazine into the brown paper bag beside him that was destined for the basement furnace.

"How could I ever? How could I?", he said softly under his

breath. A second magazine went into the bag, and then a third. That's when he came across a female name and phone number written inside a matchbook cover.

"I guess I ought to keep this," Tony mused, "don't know why, but I might need it for something some day. It's safe locked in here, besides, what will it hurt?" He used the same reasoning when he returned several other names and numbers to their hiding place.

Next Tony came to the videos. "Better be careful that I'm not throwing out anything important here," he reasoned aloud. Although the tape in his hand was labeled with a vile title that left no question about its contents, Tony headed for the VCR in the TV room--just to make sure.

He popped in the tape and then turned on the television. For just a second, before the tape started, a Christian program was being aired. " ...and people are going to hell because of it . . ." was all that Tony heard from the television before his video began. He had no idea of the spiritual battle that was taking place right then and there.

Tony viewed that video for just a bit longer than he intended. He ejected the tape, returned it to its case, picked up a second tape, and repeated the viewing process.

"Guess I'll watch just for a minute, since it's the last time I will see it before it burns," he reasoned. Tony proceeded to view the entire tape, about three hours after promising the Lord that he would throw out his entire sinful collection.

Later that afternoon, Tony's video viewing was interrupted by the familiar sound of his wife's car in the driveway. He quickly stopped and ejected the video, leaving the television playing as he ran to secure the gun box. As Tony dashed from the TV room, an old song that was one of his favorites was being sung: "...free from your burden of sin. Free at last..."

"Hey," Tony greeted, "did my two favorite girls have fun?"

"We had a blast," Deborah answered, "wait 'til you see what we got."

"Not so fast, those things are for Christmas," came Dee's response as she headed to stash away her gifts.

Tony continued to watch the television, just as if that Christian programming had been on all afternoon. He lost track of Dee for the next half hour, until she called out to Deborah from the bedroom.

"Deb, why don't you go down the street and see what the twins are doing?" Dee's voice sounded strained, but Tony reasoned that she must be tired from walking the mall.

A few seconds after the slamming of the front door announced Deborah's exit, Dee walked briskly into the room, took a stand between Tony and the television and saying nothing, dumped the contents of a brown grocery bag onto the floor, spilling her husband's entire pornography collection.

Tony's secret sin was a secret no longer. In his haste to hide that filth when he heard Dee's car, Tony had forgotten to lock his gun box. Dee, looking in the back of the closet for a place to conceal Christmas gifts for her family, had noticed that the door of the gun box was ajar. She attempted to close it, but the box was too full to even close.

For a moment no one spoke. Then Dee began to speak, but as someone with no air in her lungs. With a gasping voice, she attempted to scream.

"Who is Ginger? ... and Tassie? ... and Mona? ... Who? Who are they, Tony?" Dee was too upset to even let out a decent scream.

"I ... I ... It's ... They're ... I can explain." Tony, likewise, had no voice. His blood pressure surged. He was afraid that he was going to pass out, and then he was afraid that he wouldn't.

Although Tony had said that he could explain the material that was spread in front of him, he did not even try to do so. The excuses that he offered up during the heated exchange that followed were the same that are used by every man when his sexual addiction is brought to light: "If you were the wife I needed, I wouldn't be looking at this stuff;" ... "Those are only pictures;" ... "It makes our bedroom life better;" ... "I appreciate you more after I see these;" ... and the classic of classic excuses, "Everyone is doing it."

How much differently things would have turned out for the Taylors if Tony had been able, even at that point, to confess (in general terms) his sin to his wife, confess his sin (in specific terms) to the Lord God, to repent, to seek help for his problem, and to make himself accountable to another man for his future actions.

How much differently things would have turned out for the Taylors if Dee had known how to fight the spiritual battle against the demonic spirit of pornography that had taken her husband captive. Yes, her marriage was damaged, but it was not beyond repair.

Instead of confessions and binding against strongholds, the Taylors did battle in the flesh for the next few minutes. Dee unloaded everything that she was holding against Tony. He became so livid that he spilled the beans (that's not confession!) about his trips across the river. Tony screamed details of sexual encounters at his wife, who was already dying inside.

Tony must have felt like a trapped animal. He was exploding with rage. Dee screamed back, "I want a divorce! I want a divorce! I want a divorce!" over and over again. That's when it happened. Tony's calloused mechanic's hand folded into a fist and he struck his wife for the first time ever. Dee's breath was taken away, and she fell to the floor. Tony said nothing, but walked to their bedroom, gathered up a few personal items, and went out the front door to sit by the street and wait for John to return his car.

Dee was sitting on the floor, picking up Tony's pornography when he walked out. She did not even look at him, but continued on with her task. In a few minutes she was standing in the basement, adding great sobs to the roar of the furnace that was consuming everything she had found.

"Hey Mom!" John yelled from the top of the stairs. "What's up with Dad? He was waiting out front for me and said that he had to go somewhere. You guys gettin' divorced or something?"

Having heard her son over the roar of the furnace, Dee could not distinguish if he was simply making a joke, or if he was serious. "No, everything's all right," she replied, while wiping tears from her face in case John came down to the basement.

She could hear John's footsteps on the hardwood floor as he walked to his room. Dee busied herself for the next half hour folding clothes, while she contemplated what to do. Call the police? Go next door to the Humphries? Find an attorney? Move her and the children out of the home? Not once did she consider what should have been her first choice: Calling on the Lord she knew so well for His help and direction. In fact, she did not even consider calling on Frances, her prayer partner, who had prayed the Taylors through so many other crises. It is strange that when physical problems come to a family, God is the first one called upon, but when marriage problems come, He is often the last to be called upon.

While Dee was folding clothes, she heard the furnace click

off, bringing a small degree of closure to all that she had discovered that afternoon. By this time, she had decided to call Mary Humphries and ask for the name of the attorney who had handled her divorce from her first husband. Not even for a second did she consider that the Humphries were not Christians, and that she was about to follow the world's advice for her marriage problems. The enemy had her deceived already.

Way to go, satan. You might have won this battle, but you will not win the spiritual war for this family, precious to God.

CHAPTER 5

After leaving his home that Sunday afternoon in November, Tony drove around and thought. He did not know which way to go. He would come to an intersection and just not know which way to turn. At dusk he stopped at a convenience store, went inside and purchased what was to be his dinner: a cup of very old coffee and a chili dog. While Tony was checking out, he spotted the magazine rack behind the counter. He was jolted to reality when he realized that he had owned every magazine there.

"Need a magazine?" the clerk asked, seeing Tony eyeing the rack.

"No, not today. Maybe next time."

Tony sat in his car in front of the store eating that chili dog and sipping coffee. A car pulled in next to him with a family obviously on their way to Sunday night church. While the man went inside to make his purchase, Tony glanced at the other occupants. In the front seat was a woman he assumed to be the wife. She looked happy, giggling over the seat with two kids in the back.

Huge tears welled up in Tony's eyes as he thought about his own family. About six hours before, this could have been his family, on the way home from church. In that brief time, things had changed so much. Here he sat, eating Sunday supper in his car, not knowing where he would spend the night. He had walked out on the wife that he had abused. His secret collection of pornography had been dumped on the floor of their home in front of the coffee table, in the exact spot where he and Dee had knelt so often to pray together.

Tony knew that he had to make things right. He climbed out of the car, walked to the phone that hung inside the store, and called home. While waiting for someone to answer, he looked for the second time at that magazine rack. "Did that stuff cause all this to happen?" Tony asked himself under his breath. "Naw," he reasoned, "it's harmless. I have trouble because I have a nosy wife."

"Hello," Dee answered in a weak voice. Tony could tell that she had been crying.

"Honey, I'm so sorry — about everything."

"Tony, I can't talk to you. Please don't call again.", Dee responded to her husband.

"But what are we ...." Tony's question had been cut off by a phone being hung up. He called back, once, twice, three times, but no one answered.

A frightened Tony walked back to his car, shoulders drooping, and sobbing openly. What should he do? Where should he go? Dee Taylor had gone to her neighbor's home as soon as the pornography had finished being destroyed. She had told Mary what had happened and asked for the name of her attorney.

When satan has a message for us, he seems to always have a messenger around. Mary offered to call J. William Godalson at home and introduce Dee to him.

"You will really like this guy," Mary chatted while looking for the attorney's home phone number. "He's sharp and he gets things done fast. His speciality is divorce and he really goes for the throat."

"Goes for the throat?" Dee repeated. "I don't want anyone going for my husband's throat. I only want someone to make all this stuff go away."

"Hey, it's only a saying. These guys need to be shaken to wake them up and he really knows how to shake them."

Mr. Godalson provided the sympathetic ear that Dee had needed that afternoon. He allowed her to tell the entire story, interjecting an authoritative-sounding "yes" several times along the way. Only after she had finished, did he offer any comment of substance.

"I need you to come in early tomorrow, say about 9:30," the attorney counseled, "and we'll get things started for you. Mary can give you my address. My standard retainer for a divorce is $4,000 and you will need to bring a check with you. Until we meet, I want you to have no contact in person or by phone with your husband," he concluded.

Dee thought about his comments, as well as those of Mary, as she walked across the lawn to her home. "Go for the throat--shake her husband--divorce--no contact," Dee mumbled under her breath. "Something just doesn't seem right, but I guess all that has happened isn't right either."

Although it was almost December, there must have been leaves remaining on the huge oak tree that grew between the Taylor's home and the Humphries'. Just as Dee walked under it, a leaf fell and lodged between her glasses and her eyebrow. It was almost as though God was calling out from the heavens, "You haven't asked for my help yet. I am the One that made the two of you one-flesh in marriage and I am the only One who can really heal a hurting marriage." Not realizing that leaf could have come from the Trinity instead of from the tree, Dee pulled if from her face and cast it aside.

Attorney Godalson had provided the sympathetic ear that Dee had needed. There was someone else who also would have had a sympathetic ear, her prayer partner, Frances. Much like that attorney had done, Frances would have interjected an affirming "yes" along the way as Dee told her story. Her "yes" would have been said not with authority, but with compassion.

There was one huge difference between the listening ear of Frances and the ear of an attorney. Frances had the ear of God, but not once that afternoon did Dee even think about calling her. The deceiver had indeed come to the Taylor home to work his evil schemes. Who would stand against him, in the power of the name of Jesus?

CHAPTER 6

You might have heard that it is unwise to purchase a new automobile that was assembled on a Monday, for that is when the most mistakes are made. In Paducah, it would also have been unwise to have had your car repaired on a Monday by Tony Taylor. He went through the motions of working and repairing cars, but his thoughts were somewhere else.

Tony had spent Sunday night sleeping in his automobile. Although he could have used his credit card and gone to a motel, it must have been self-punishment that caused him to forego a decent place of rest.

Sunday evening, after observing that family at the convenience store, and after having his wife hang up on him on the phone, Tony sunk to a level of despair that he would come to experience frequently in the days ahead. Sitting in front of the store, Tony wished that he had one of his guns with him.

"If I blew my brains all over this car, my problems would be over. Then Dee would notice me. That would make her sorry for hanging up on me," Tony had reasoned illogically. He did not know that the prayers of Frances and of his praying grandmother would prohibit him from ever harming himself.

Late Sunday evening, Tony had driven to his shop. He backed his car in next to a row of used cars and had slept there unnoticed. His sleep had been fitful. Several times he had awakened. Each time it would only take a second for him to remember why he was sleeping in the car. Each time that realization had been followed by almost unbearable panic. The enemy had Tony so deceived that not even once during that difficult night did he consider seeking help from the Lord God, whom he had served so faithfully until a few months prior.

Monday morning Tony had attempted to freshen up in the

locker room at work. The cup of coffee that he called breakfast was far different from the one that he would have had at home, sitting at the table with Dee. How Tony wished he could hear her pray for him on this morning, as she often did before he left for work.

"Hey, Preacher Man, what's wrong with you today?" Mitch called out to Tony several times that day from the adjoining work station. "Something's up with you. I just know it. What's happening?"

"Nothing," Tony had lied. "Just a Monday with a lot on my mind."

Mitch had worked next to Tony for almost a year. They were not close friends, but did talk every day, usually about automobiles or sports. He had gone through a divorce about six months before and now lived in a trailer in West Paducah. Mitch had resisted every one of Tony's attempts to share the good news of Jesus Christ with him, back in the days when Tony was walking with the Lord. Tony suspected that Mitch was behind the locker photo incident.

That day at lunch, instead of eating a sandwich packed by his wife, and finding a love note from her packed inside, Tony ate a sandwich purchased from the "roach coach" as the men called it, that pulled into the garage each day at noon. On this Monday, Tony did not eat in his car, nor did he take his Bible and read it while sitting alone. He ate with the other men, and listened to their boasts of weekend sexual conquests. Mitch seemed to be the most boastful of the group, sparing them no details.

Some of the tingle that pornography had given Tony now returned to him in a different way. One of the men told a pornographic joke, with his own wife as the object, and all the men laughed. Tony laughed loudest of all.

"Look at this," Mitch exclaimed, "Preacher Man is human after all. What happened to you this weekend, Preacher Man?" When Tony did not reply, Mitch offered a vile and obscene guess at what had brought about the change in Tony. Every man there exploded with laughter. In his mind, Tony imagined what had just been described, and that newfound tingle came back again.

Had that incident taken place six months before, Tony would have offered the most Christlike rebuke that he could provide. He would have silently prayed and would have forgiven the men involved, praying for their salvation. He would have asked the Lord to remove the comment from his mind.

There had been a lot of changes. On this Monday afternoon, Tony allowed that thought to come back time and time again, until the image had passed from his head to his heart. Over the next few days, he would allow that thought to make its progression from his heart to his hand, as he acted out what had begun as an off-color joke.

That afternoon, just before quitting time, Tony noticed the brown uniform of a sheriff's deputy at the service manager's work station. This wasn't unusual, for the shop often worked on their fleet, and they would pick up cars about this time of day.

With his head under the hood of a car, Tony was not aware of the man standing next to him, until he spoke.

"Are you William Anthony Taylor?"

The question startled Tony, for no one, except for his family, knew his full name. He raised up to find the words were being spoken by the deputy.

"Yes. Yes, I am," Tony stuttered.

"I am serving you with an Order for Protection, petitioned from the court by Delores Ramsey Taylor. You are prohibited, under penalty of law, from going within one thousand feet of the petitioner. You are prohibited from making any attempt to contact her by telephone or mail."

"Wha-What does this mean?" Tony questioned.

"It means that if you go around this woman, or disturb her in any way, you will go to jail."

The deputy was gone as quickly as he had arrived. Tony stood alone, leaning on his tool box, holding a court order in his grease-covered hand. He was too shocked to cry, scream, or even move. He had assumed that he would go home after work and apologize to Dee. They would cry together. They would possibly pray together. She would apologize for causing his self-inflicted punishment of sleeping in the car.

Had things happened that way, Tony would someday have found another place to hide his pornography. Without question, he would have been going across the bridge again shortly thereafter. The stronghold of sexual addiction in Tony's spirit would not have been dealt with, and at some point, satan would have caused it to surface again.

"Bummer man, having your old lady do that to you. Sorry for you, Preacher Man," Mitch consoled in his own crude way. "I knew something was up when you came to work without shaving. Then you ate lunch with the guys and laughed with us. Where you gonna live?"

"Where am I going to live?" Tony repeated. That is when fear set in.

He had only one change of clothes with him and only a few personal items. Now the court wouldn't even allow him to go home! Where would he live?

"Preacher Man, there is a second bedroom in my trailer. Why don't you use it for a while? It might do me some good to be around someone 'holy'."

Suddenly, Tony felt as filthy on the inside as the greasy hand tightly grasping his Order. "This vile man thought I was 'holy' and I am no better than he is. I have failed God and I have failed my family. I give up trying to be a Christian. It doesn't work."

That morning, Mary Humphries had driven Dee to the attorney's office. On the way, Dee stopped at the bank, where she depleted almost all of the Taylor's savings. She also had to cash the Christmas club check they had just received.

"It sure won't be much of a Christmas for the kids this year," she confessed to Mary. "They have no dad, and now there is no money for Christmas either." Sunglasses concealed her eyes, swollen from crying all night.

Well, you are right and wrong, Mrs. Taylor. Your children do have a father. In fact, they have two fathers. They have an earthly father needing prayers for his release from the enemy's captivity. They also have a heavenly Father, ready to meet your every need. We cannot release Tony, nor can you. What we can do is pray that the Lord would reveal strongholds. We can pray for your husband to be set free to be the man, the husband, the father, and the child of God, that Tony was created to be. Jesus died so that your Tony could live, not in a hollow, sin-filled life, but victorious over all that has him enslaved.

You are also right, Mrs. Taylor when you say there will be no money for Christmas. There is not money because you are about to pay an attorney, but that is only a symptom of the real problem. You see, when the enemy starts attacking a family, he does not stop with only destroying the marriage. The evil one will attack that family's finances. So often in the process he also attacks the health of someone in that precious family. His attack might also reach to the children in that home. They rebel, or leave home, or become involved in drugs. If the enemy was not stopped by Dee fighting the spiritual battle for her husband, it is quite predictable that he would continue to attack more and more areas of her life.

You might be wondering why satan singled out the Taylor family for his attack. Why not the Humphries next door? Or someone down the street? Satan is intent on destroying any family or individual with the ability to accomplish great things for the cause of Christ. Consider all that the Taylors had already been carrying out for the Lord, with their musical talents, Tony's witness at work, and the raising of two Christian children. John had talked to his parents about the leading he was feeling to become a missionary. This family had to be stopped by the prince of darkness.

The Humphries posed no threat, for they were already living for satan. They never went to church. Alcohol was used in the home on a regular basis. Don Humphries had given Dee an eerie feeling one day when she had been alone with him in her kitchen. She suspected that he was already being unfaithful to Mary, his new wife.

If a burglar was intent on entering your home today, he would first look for an open door. When the evil one became intent on destroying the Taylors, he looked for an open door. He found that door in Tony's life through pornography.

Dee did not know about it, and Tony did not think much about it, but that door had been opened to pornography when Tony was twelve years old. One summer afternoon, he and his buddy Calvin had been exploring the woods behind Calvin's home. There was a rural road on the opposite side of the woods that people used for their dumping grounds. Tony and Calvin always had to explore what had been left there.

On that summer afternoon, they had discovered a new pile

of debris. While searching through it, Tony had discovered a girlie magazine. Neither of those two boys had ever seen a naked female body before. The event that we have been calling "Tony's thrill" was first experienced by him on that day.

Both young boys were at first speechless as they turned the pages and stared at photo after photo. They began to make comments to each other about the photos and the females in them. It wasn't long before Tony said, "Let's search. There might be more." His progressive addiction to pornography had just kicked in, when that one magazine no longer satisfied, and he wanted more.

On that day, the card file in hell must have recorded Tony's potential stronghold. Years later, when Tony's Christian family had to be brought down, the enemy did not have to search for a way to come in. Tony had left a door open since his childhood.

On the afternoon of the big discovery, Tony and Calvin had indeed found more magazines, some of which would be pornographic by anyone's standards today. The boys made a fort in the woods where their magazines were carefully concealed.

That evening at home, Tony could not look his mother in the eye. He felt guilty because of what he had discovered, but he wanted to see more. The next day, the boys returned to their fort. This continued all summer. Along the way, they invited a couple other boys into their "club." Their society disbanded one day when a father came looking for his son and discovered what was taking place. He promptly destroyed the magazines, but those images would live for decades in Tony's mind.

From that day until Tony opened his life to Christ at age twenty, he continued to dabble in pornography. No one on earth knew about his secret sin. Tony would purchase a new magazine and experience that thrill. It wasn't long until he needed new images to satisfy him.

On the day that Tony discovered the difference that Jesus Christ can make in a life, he promised the Lord that he was through with filth.

Tony was promising the Lord what he intended to do, without asking the Lord for His help with the problem. Tony was as serious about his commitment as anyone has ever been. The only problem, however, was that Tony was attempting in his own strength to clean up that area of his life. He already had a bondage that needed to be broken.

Even after he and Dee were married, striving to live for the Lord, Tony would from time to time, have an opportunity to reopen the door to his bondage. Dee knew nothing about her husband's futile struggle to live clean in that one area of his life.

Shortly after John was born, the dealership where Tony worked sent him to the automobile factory in Detroit for a three day seminar on air bags. Kissing his wife good-bye, as she held their new son in the doorway of their home, the idea of being unfaithful to his wife on that trip was far from his mind.

"I'll be praying for you," Dee called out as Tony got into his car, heading for the airport. Unfortunately, being busy caring for a new baby consumed Dee's time, and that promise was forgotten. She did not once bring her husband's name before the Lord for those next three days.

Tony first flew from Barkley Field in Paducah to St. Louis on a commuter flight. There he boarded the largest plane that he had ever seen for a flight to Detroit. Once the plane was in the air, Tony began to explore the seat pocket in front of him. He discovered that someone had left a magazine there. Although it was one of the slick, well-done publications accepted by the world, a Christian would consider it pornography.

Tony looked around the cabin. Away from home, with no one he knew, Tony opened the magazine. He began to turn page after page. The man in the seat next to him glanced at what he was reading and offered a vile comment about one female. Suddenly, Tony thought that he was back in the woods with Calvin. He felt guilty, but he continued looking and reading.

During the first day of his seminar, Tony thought often about the airbrushed-to-perfection bodies that he had observed in the magazine on the plane. He thought about purchasing a magazine that evening. "I'm a thousand miles from home, and no one will know," Tony thought as if attempting to convince himself. "Besides, what does it hurt. They are only pictures."

Wrong, Tony, wrong. Each picture is of a young lady, for whom our Lord Jesus gave His life. That girl smiling at you from the magazine page has been a cooing infant smiling back at her mama and daddy. She has been a precious toddler forming words through innocent lips. She might have been the little girl who learned to sing 'Jesus Loves Me' as her first song. She could have been a girl who ran home so excited when she had her first boyfriend. She was the girl who brought home report cards with good grades on them. She was the sixteen year old who someone taught to drive the family car.

She is now the young lady who is breaking her family's heart. She is the young lady whose grandma cries out to God hour after hour, asking Him to save her prodigal and to deliver her from a life of sin. She is the young lady that is so precious to God and to her family. And you, Tony Taylor, want to see the body that the Lord has given her, so that you can become aroused. How dare you, Tony Taylor, how dare you? May God have mercy on you.

That evening after his seminar, Tony did not purchase a sinful magazine. He only needed to reach for the TV remote control in his hotel room to have access to the most vile filth imaginable. To Tony Taylor, the sex addict, that one magazine on the plane had been much like one drink to an alcoholic. It only created the need for more and more.

"What does it hurt, you ask?" Here it is fifteen years later and Tony's wife is on the way to an attorney's office. Pornography doesn't just hurt, it kills families.

That morning, Attorney J. William Godalson scribbled on a legal pad while asking Dee questions about her marriage and family.

"Has he ever struck you?" Mr. Godalson inquired.

"Yesterday afternoon was the first time. I guess that was my fault for confronting him."

"Where did he hit you? How many times? How hard?"

"Just once, in my stomach. I don't know how hard. It knocked the wind out of me, but I was screaming at the same time. It was more like a shove than a punch. Can't we just forget about that?"

Mr. Godalson did not respond, but continued to write on the legal pad that lay before him. He reached for his telephone intercom, pressed the buzzer twice, and tore a sheet off of the pad. A few seconds later, his secretary entered the office and he gave her the sheet of paper.

"Here's what I want you to do," the attorney counseled. "Go home and close all your credit card accounts. Transfer any monies in your checking account into a new account created in your name only. I trust you brought the retainer fee in a cashier's check as requested. As I told you on the phone yesterday, have no contact with Mr. Taylor. As soon as we are notified who his attorney is, I will communicate with him. I want to get you in the best position possible."

"The best position for what?", Dee asked with a puzzled look on her face.

"The best position for court, in case Mr. Taylor contests the divorce," came the reply. "Most of these rascals just roll over and die when we put the screws to them. Don't worry, though. You are a victim of abuse. We're all set."

"I'm all set for what?", Dee fired back, repeating her attorney's last comment. It suddenly struck Dee that she was about to set the wheels in motion that would end her marriage. Even after all she discovered in the last 24 hours, something (or Someone) just told her that she was making a mistake.

Attorney Godalson leaned back, sighing, as his desk chair let out a squeak. He was obviously disturbed that Dee was questioning what was happening. "I am a divorce attorney and you are an abuse victim. I am here to help you, but you need to follow my counsel. Of course, you are welcome to walk out the door and forget that we ever met."

Dee noticed that the cashier's check for $4,000 had suddenly disappeared from the desk. "Maybe he could forget that we met, but I would have a $4,000 reminder," she thought.

Mr. Godalson leaned forward, causing his chair to squeak again. He displayed a stern look and pointed his index finger at Dee as he began to speak. "I do need to warn you of what might happen, though. I would suspect that by now Mr. Taylor has consulted an attorney..."

"Why does he call Tony, Mr. Taylor, and not my husband?" Dee wondered.

"... if you fail to act, he will get the upper hand. Let me run some words by you: child abduction... molestation... foreclosure... bankruptcy. Leopards don't change their spots, and once a marriage goes bad, nothing can bring it back. Yours is dead, so let's bury it. If you fail to carry out what needs to be done, I will in no way be liable for anything that happens."

"Dee, I know how you feel," said Mary, the neighbor who had chauffeured Dee to the appointment. "Remember, I went through the same things. It's natural to be scared. I promise you, Bill can take away a lot of the pain. Besides, when you get what you are entitled to, you'll feel that you have gotten even with Tony for betraying and abusing you."

"You must be right," Dee said, attempting not to cry. Something about everything that was happening just didn't feel right to her. She noticed the secretary had returned to the room and had handed a document to the attorney.

"I'll just need you to sign this paper for me," he requested, handing Dee a pen.

Dee read PETITION FOR ORDER OF PROTECTION typed across the top of the page in large letters.

"What's this?", she asked.

"Just routine. It's something done to protect you. I will get a copy to you as soon as it has been ordered."

"When will I stop being so stunned and scared?", Dee asked no one in particular.

"It's all downhill from here," her attorney replied.

He was correct. The destruction of another precious marriage was indeed about to go downhill all the way from here.

Late that afternoon, Dee was surprised to have a messenger deliver an envelope to her from the office of J. William Godalson. Opening it, she found an Order for Protection issued by the court. Tony was not allowed to contact her or to come within 1,000 feet of her. Dee was shocked to read the statement she had signed earlier in the day. It read as though Tony had beaten her within an inch of her life, and that she was afraid he would return and kill her.

"Tony is not a monster," she sobbed. "He's my husband who made a bad mistake. No one wants to help us. I don't need an Order for Protection, I need help!"

Holding the court order in her hand, she cried out, "If we could only talk, I know we could work this all out."

At the same time, a brokenhearted mechanic clutched the same document and thought to himself, "If we could only talk, I know we could work this all out."

No one can know the thoughts of the Lord, apart from how He reveals Himself to us in His Word, the Bible. We suspect that at the same time, from the portals of heaven, a holy God was asking, "Why don't they seek My help? I am The Protector."

CHAPTER 7

"Alpha 41, 10-56. The man, Lone Oak Road at Lincoln, reference a moving detail, 1725 hours," the police radio crackled. *"Alpha 42, back him."*

Before leaving work, Tony had called the Sheriff's Department to see how he could get his things out of his home without risking going to jail. They explained to him that an officer had to accompany him.

"Call back when you are down the street from your home," the police dispatcher advised. "Tell them you have a 'moving detail' and we will send an officer." It had become so common for a spouse needing help from the police to move out of their home that it had picked up the "moving detail" label. That event became violent so often that two officers were always dispatched.

Tony was embarrassed as he drove down his street, with two police cars following him. The dispatcher had called Dee and advised her what was about to happen. She had been requested to unlock the front door and then to remain in a far bedroom until her husband left.

Once inside the home, one officer tapped on the closed door of John's room and identified himself to Dee. The second officer cautioned Tony not to remove anything that was not his own, and not to destroy any property. He then followed one step behind Tony everywhere he went.

Tony did not know where to start. He wandered into the couple's bedroom and began to drop clothing and personal items into one of the large garbage bags that he had been instructed by the police to bring with him. As he emptied his closet, the gun box became visible back in the corner. It had been left open. As Tony took his key ring from his pocket and bent forward to lock that box, he took notice of how empty it appeared. He knew why it was vacant and the reason it was open.

The Lord had lessons to teach Tony about strongholds that he was far from ready to learn. As he was preparing to leave his home for what he thought might be the last time, under the watchful eye of a lawman, he knew the answer to his open-ended question about pornography: "What does it hurt?"

As Tony moved to his dresser, he noticed the area on top where Dee used to leave notes for him. He spotted an envelope with his name written in Dee's characteristic handwriting. "This is it!", he thought while tearing the envelope open. "It's from Dee and this nightmare is over!" Inside the envelope, Tony found five crisp one hundred dollar bills. There was no note inside, only the money.

Tony started across the house to the door where the second policeman stood watch. He stopped short when he realized the officer was not moving. "Sir, don't go there, unless you want to go to jail," he ordered.

"But my wife left me some money, and there is not a note or anything. I need to know what it means."

"You cannot talk to her."

"Man, have a heart. Don't you have a wife? What if someone did this to you? Please, I need to see her. She left me some money and I don't know what it means. Help me out, please, I just need to ask her one question."

"I'm sorry, but your wife has a protection order against you and I can't allow you to speak to her. Please talk to your attorney. We can only stay here 20 minutes, so you best get your things together now."

Dee, sitting on the edge of her son's bed behind the closed door, heard her husband's desperate pleas to see her, and it broke her heart. He was moving out and she had no idea where he was going. She did not know where he had slept the night before. Deborah had cried herself to sleep last night, and John was threatening to run away

.

Dee began to sob uncontrollably. For the first time during the past 24 hours of horror, she called on the name of Jesus for help. Her prayer wasn't eloquent, but it did reach our Lord, who the Bible promises hears every uttering and groaning of our heart.

"Mrs. Taylor, we are leaving now. I will secure your front door," one of the officers called through the closed bedroom door.

"Thank you," Dee replied, interrupting her praying.

"Thank you?", she thought. "You just moved my husband out of the house and I say 'Thank you?' What is wrong with me? I am going crazy."

Dee hurried from the bedroom, hoping to catch a glimpse of Tony. She pulled back the front drapes and peered through a small gap. Tony was standing next to his car, loading plastic bags into the back seat. His shirttail was out and his shoulders were stooped. Her Tony looked tired. How badly she wanted to run out the front door, give him a hug, and ask what sounded good for dinner. No doubt he would have a cute anecdote to share with his wife about his day.

Just as Tony loaded the last bag, one of the officers drove away. The other was standing beside Tony, in the near-darkness, chatting with him. How much Dee wished she could hear what they were saying. Her spirits were lifted about one percent when she saw Tony extend his hand to shake with the officer, and a small smile came to his face. It was not an

"I'm happy" smile, but an "I'm all right" smile.

Had Dee been able to hear that conversation, she would have heard Tony ask if the officer knew of a state policeman named Tremonte.

"Yessir, I do," the officer answered.

"I think I need to contact him," Tony replied.

"It would be inappropriate for me to comment, under the circumstances, but, yes, I have talked to him," the officer had replied while giving Tony a knowing wink. That's what had caused Tony to smile.

Dee allowed the drapes to close, and began to fix dinner for herself and Deborah. Deborah had been doing homework in the basement and did not even know that her dad had been there. On an impulse, Dee went into her bedroom, hoping that Tony had left a note, or an address, or anything for her.

Everywhere she looked, all she could see was evidence of Tony having moved out. His half of the closet was empty. His dresser was empty, as was his night stand. He had even taken his pillow. His well-worn Bible had been left behind.

On the way to find Mitch's trailer, at an address in West Paducah that would soon be his home, Tony stopped at their bank to deposit $400 of the $500 that Dee had left for him, just in case Dee needed extra money. After inserting his bank card and entering his PIN number, a report came on the screen, "ACCOUNT CLOSED - CARD RETAINED."

"That's just great," Tony mumbled to the machine. "My wife kicks me out and now you make a mistake and eat my card. What could happen to me next?" It would only take Tony about fifteen minutes to find out.

On the way out of town, Tony stopped for gas. His gas charge card was declined. Then he attempted to use his credit card. The clerk was soon on the phone to the credit card company, and his card was confiscated, as the account had been closed. He attempted to pay for his gas with one of the $100 bills, but the clerk pointed to a sign that read "NO $100 BILLS ACCEPTED". Tony finally came up with the $14.72 for gas by pooling his money with coins from the console of his car.

After the delays, it was pitch dark when Tony finally located Mitch's trailer. The trailer had seen its better days. "Didn't know that I was going to be living with Rockford," he mumbled as he exited his car, recalling one of his favorite television programs.

After knocking on the door, Mitch answered, barefoot and shirtless, even in the cold night air. He had a beer in his hand. "Come on in, Preacher Man. I thought that you might have had a better offer on the way," he joked.

Tony was stunned, to say the least, by what he first saw when he entered the bachelor trailer. Unlike his home, which Dee had always maintained in immaculate condition, the living room of the trailer looked as though it had not been cleaned since Rockford moved out.

There were piles of old newspapers, and rows of empty beer bottles. On the coffee table was a casket-shaped container. Next to it sat a stack of pornographic magazines. Dust upon dust covered everything.

Tony hoped that his shock had not shown, but even if it had, Mitch was in no condition to notice. Although Tony did not consider himself to be a prodigal, he had indeed moved into the pig pen.

Tony was exhausted, due to his prior sleepless night, combined with the emotion of all that was happening. He lugged his possessions into the small second bedroom of that trailer, took a shower, and went to bed. It only took him a minute to fall asleep, but even during that time, he could smell Dee's hair on the pillow that he had brought from home. Tony fell asleep with tears in his closed eyes.

Although Tony missed his family very badly, he did adjust to his new living arrangements in a few days. Mitch suddenly became his best friend. They rode back and forth to work together. During the day, Mitch would chat with Tony while they worked.

That evening when Tony had first moved in, it bothered him that Mitch had called him "Preacher Man," but by the end of that first week, he was hearing it so often that it almost went without notice.

There was one incident though, when Tony was working on a car. The job was routine, and with his mind wandering, he began to recall some of the pictures that he had viewed the night before in the magazines on Mitch's coffee table.

"Hey, Preacher Man, what do you wanna do for supper?", Mitch called out from the adjoining work station.

"Preacher Man?", Tony had thought, "He ought to be calling me 'Sinner Man' from the way that I am living." That thought might well have been one of the first of many of God's attempts to get Tony's attention. It did not matter that Tony had not listened, for we serve a God who will not give up on one of His lost sheep. The Bible assures us that He will leave the ninety nine safe sheep to go find the one lost sheep.

Although Dee was trying so hard to give up on Tony, God was not. He was also going to convict Dee that she should not be giving up. Dee had listened to what others said she should do about her marriage problems, but she had not asked the Lord.

"How about fried chicken?", Tony yelled back above the noise of a dozen mechanics at work. "I saw some in the roach coach at noon. It looked good and it got me thinking about it. I know where we can pick up fried chicken and cornbread on the way home."

That evening, the two new best buddies sat in the living room of Rockford's trailer, still wearing their soiled uniforms, and ate fried chicken with their hands.

"Want something to drink?", Mitch asked.

"Yeah, this cornbread is kinda dry."

Mitch went across the room to the refrigerator and pulled out two bottles of beer. Tony was surprised when Mitch handed him one. Not wanting to offend the one who was providing him a place to live, he began to drink it. At that moment, Tony did not, even for one second, consider that he was offending the One who had given him life, his precious Lord God.

That first sip of beer had been distasteful, but it washed down dinner, and Tony drank until the bottle was empty. In a few minutes, Mitch pulled out two more bottles. The television program they were watching became real funny to Tony, especially after the third bottle of beer.

Tony had forgotten at that moment, that his father had been an alcoholic and died when Tony was ten years old, as the result of his drinking. Although he did not know about generational curses, Tony had always vowed to Dee that he would never touch alcoholic beverages.

Tony had been too young to know it when his dad had died, and his mom had never told him, but the senior Mr. Taylor had been repeatedly unfaithful to Tony's mom. Many nights he would drink himself into a stupor and not even come home. Both of Tony's parents had died without knowing the

Lord.

Tony's sexual addiction was a generational curse passed down from his father. As a result of that curse, a second curse of alcoholism was about to manifest itself in his life. Left unchecked, both of those curses were about to pass on to another generation. Tony's son, John, who had sensed a call to be a missionary, had begun to secretly dabble in pornography.

One day a few months prior, John had used his dad's car. A friend had a dead battery and he had been searching in his dad's trunk for jumper cables. It was then that he discovered the first magazine that Tony had hidden behind the spare tire. Since that time, John had a book of his own hidden away in his room where no one would ever find it. Recently, though, he had found his original book boring and wanted one with more graphic photographs.

"Ready for dessert, Preacher Man?", Mitch asked of his dinner companion.

"Sure, what are we having?"

"My specialty!", Mitch responded, as he opened the small wooden casket that sat on the coffee table in front of the two men. It appeared to contain a strange form of tobacco.

"What's that?", Tony asked innocently.

"It's the best pot ever grown in western Kentucky!", Mitch answered, while carefully placing a pinch of the substance into cigarette wrapping paper. He handed it to Tony and offered a lighter to him.

With his senses dulled by the beer, Tony began to smoke the strange cigarette. In a few minutes, his situation seemed not quite as bleak.

"Know what, good buddy?" he mumbled to the man next to him. "My old lady dumping me is the best thing that has ever happened to me. Man, this is the life!"

Tony awoke to sunlight coming in the window of the trailer. It took him a few seconds to remember where he was and what had happened. He had spent the night on the sofa, still wearing his soiled work clothes from the day before. His head ached and he was too stiff to even move. Since it was Friday, he called in sick, and Mitch left for work alone.

Tony spent the day sleeping, and unpacking his belongings, in a futile attempt to create a home in the small room where he found himself living. For the first time since last Monday, he had slowed down long enough to recall just how much he missed his family. He wanted to be home, but there was nothing that he could do. Tony consoled himself with the stack of magazines from the coffee table.

Late that afternoon, he heard someone opening the front door and was surprised to see an overweight red-haired woman entering the trailer. She appeared rough, and carried a suitcase and bag of groceries.

"Hi! I'm Margie. Who are you?", she inquired.

"I'm Tony."

"I'm glad to meet you. Seems like Mitch is forever bringing home a stray."

Tony had no idea who this woman might be, but she carried herself as though she had been in that trailer many times before. He sensed that he was intruding on her space.

"From the look on your face, I guess Mitch forgot to tell you about me. I'm his girlfriend, or common law wife, or something. I work in Lexington and come here on the weekends to get Mitch straightened out. That's about the only time he eats a real meal. How many cases of beer did you guys go through this week?"

Tony did not respond. He barely heard the question, because he was busy thinking about how far wrong his life had gone in only six days. Tony was thankful that Mitch arrived home from work only a few minutes later.

"Preacher Man, I brought some stuff for you," Mitch reported. He handed Tony his weekly paycheck and a large manila envelope. It bore no return name, but had the Taylor's address. The envelope was addressed to Tony at work, in Dee's handwriting. Tony tore it open with anticipation. Inside he found mail that Dee was forwarding to him. There was also a note from her, in which she asked for his address. The note also explained that her attorney said to close their bank account and cancel the credit cards. Dee added that she had left the $500 to help him out. Before, she had always signed her notes "Love ya, Dee" or something. This note was signed "Dee Taylor," as if Tony had more than one Dee asking for his address.

Although Margie had brought groceries and fixed both men a great dinner, Tony felt as though he would suffocate for the balance of the evening. The drinking and drugs were all too much for him. At one point, he walked outside into the cold, Kentucky, December night air. With his back to the trailer, Tony looked up into the sky. It was a clear night and the stars shown brightly.

"God, if You are up there, why am I in such a mess?" he pleaded. Tony did not wait for the Lord to answer, but walked back into his den of sin.

CHAPTER 8

Tony was out of the trailer Saturday morning before Mitch and Margie awoke. He went to his favorite Saturday breakfast spot and ordered pancakes. While waiting for his order, Tony wondered what might happen should Dee decide to take the children out to breakfast, and walk in the door. The image of a tearful reunion of a happy family was so vivid in his mind that Tony had to look toward the door to make certain that Dee had not actually arrived.

Dee and her children would not be seen in restaurants for quite a while. She had explained to her children the items to be cut from their budget until "your father and I work out this money thing." Dining out had been the first item to go.

Tony had told Mitch that he would be out for most of the day. As he paid for his breakfast, he glanced at his watch and saw it was only 9:00 A.M. Our friend Tony was about to experience all the loneliness and temptation of a partner in a troubled marriage.

Tony's foremost task that cold, December Saturday, was to locate a place to receive mail. He was so embarrassed at his new living arrangements that he did not want Dee to know the address. However, deep within, he wanted her to know, so that there would always be the possibility that Dee would change her mind and knock on his door. He recalled how an intoxicated and shirtless Mitch had greeted him that first evening, when he had knocked on the trailer door.

Something (or Someone) touched Tony once again, as he realized he had been living with Mitch for only five days. During that short time, he had begun to drink beer, had experimented with marijuana, and had read pornographic books that were openly displayed. The previous night, his new roommate slept with a woman who was not his wife. He suddenly felt dirtier than the basket of clothes setting on his back seat.

Yes, perhaps Dee had legally requested that he not return to their home, but in five days, he had become a prodigal. That happened not because Tony was running from his one-flesh mate, but because Tony was running from the Lord God, straight into satan's open arms.

Every stop Tony made that Saturday morning, starting with breakfast alone, was characteristic of a prodigal spouse. Since he had no bank account, he stopped at a check cashing store and cashed his pay check, paying a high fee for the privilege.

Although he had not discussed finances with Dee, Tony purchased a money order for one half of his check to send to his family. Counting the cash that had been returned to him, he mentally figured how much he would pay Mitch, and how little he would have left.

Dee would be shocked to receive that money order in Monday's mail. Nevertheless, the impact on the finances of the Taylor household would be the same as if Tony's pay had suddenly been cut by fifty percent.

Somehow, when Tony made out his mental budget, he neglected to include his tithe and offering to the Lord. Tony and Dee Taylor had testimony after testimony of the Lord's provision when they were obedient with the tithe. Even though her husband was disobedient in his giving, Dee would be giving ten percent of that money order to the Lord.

Tony then stopped at a mail box rental store. In a few minutes, he had an address, although it gave no indication of where he actually lived. Tony did not know how to get the address and money order to Dee.

"She couldn't get mad if I stopped at home to give her

money," he reasoned. The image of the officer blocking him from his wife and the threat of jail was enough for him to decide to send it by mail. Searching through a rack of cards at the mail store, Tony could not find anything that sounded right. Finally, he bought a card that he discarded, just so that he would have an envelope.

Tony stuck the money order inside the envelope, tucked in a note with his new address on it, and started to seal the envelope. It seemed odd to be addressing a letter to his own home. That was something that Tony just never had occasion to do.

Tony thought about a time he had selected just the right card to mail home. It was years before, in Detroit, while he was attending a seminar. He had become caught up in some things that a Christian man should not be doing. Early one morning, the Lord had spoken to Tony, and had even given him a special verse from the Gideon Bible in his room. On the way to the seminar, he picked out a card in the hotel's gift shop and mailed it home. Tony and Dee had a good laugh about it when Tony arrived home two days before the card did!

Just before sealing the envelope, Tony reached into the trash basket next to him, and recovered the card that he had selected. It sounded more appropriate than when he had first read it. Tony signed it, "I miss you guys, Dad", tucked in the money order, affixed a stamp, and mailed it.

On the way to his next stop of the morning, Tony sensed just a small bit of satisfaction inside, knowing how proud Dee would be of her card, even under the present circumstances. His mind raced back to that Detroit incident. He had felt so guilty and unclean over what had happened. He had also felt a peace at knowing that the Lord had forgiven him.

"That was not much, compared to all that I have done since then," Tony said aloud as he drove to his next stop. "God, if only you could make me feel that clean again."

It was indeed Tony's desire to be made clean, forgiven by the Lord. Yet, he was in the bondage of sexual addiction, causing him to be double minded. He wanted forgiveness, but he also wanted an affair.

"If Dee doesn't want me, I will find someone who does," he uttered aloud. A sordid image from one of the magazines came to Tony's mind.

How could a man who had known the Lord, verbalize wanting God to make him clean again, and then state he wants to find someone else, all in the same breath? He could want both because Tony had a battle raging within. The spirit of whoredoms had taken him captive. Who will take a stand, praying for Tony's salvation, the restoration of his family, and for his release from slavery to sin?

Tony pulled into a parking space and lifted the basket of soiled clothes from the back seat of his car. The coin laundry, warmed by the clothes dryers, relaxed Tony as soon as he stepped through the door. He separated his clothes into two machines, added coins and soap, and then looked for a spot to read the newspaper that he had found in the booth at breakfast.

Doing the laundry in this warm place made Tony feel right at home, for he washed his own work clothes every Saturday. Engrossed in reading the paper, with several machines at work, Tony had not noticed that a woman had sat down on the bench next to him.

"Excuse me, could I borrow a section of your paper?"

"Sure, take your pick."

"No sense in making them chop down a tree so that I can read the paper for a few minutes, right?"

"Sure, and besides, I have trouble reading more than a couple sections at the same time."

The woman next to Tony laughed. That made him feel good. Apart from talking to Margie for a few minutes the prior evening, it was the first time that he had conversed with a female since Dee had exploded on the prior Sunday. He felt even better than he had a few minutes before.

Although Tony was soon back into the sports section, he noticed how nice this unknown female smelled. Even above the smell of scented laundry detergent, she smelled nice. He did not move the paper, but shifted his eyes enough that he could observe her. To Tony, she looked just perfect.

At that very moment, the evil spirit within him began to manifest itself. He had thoughts that are not worth repeating.

"Did you know that you are reading yesterday's paper?", she asked. "You really do believe in saving the trees, don't you?"

"Sorry about that. I found it lying in my booth at breakfast."

"I'm no better," the stranger consoled. "I read two sections before I noticed the date. Guess neither of us have much of a life, right?"

"Wow! Is she coming on to me?", Tony silently wondered. "This is the part of being divorced that I'm looking forward to." Had that woman been able to know Tony's thoughts, she would have run out the door.

"The most exciting event of my Saturday is watching my dryer turn," he quipped in an effort to be witty.

"I know what you mean," she replied. "Is that why you do

the laundry instead of your wife?"

"I'm divorced," Tony replied with no hesitation. If he had wanted to be completely accurate, he should have said, "I am a Christian man who is away from the Lord. I also have a secret sexual addiction that I must feed at the expense of everyone around me. I am not divorced, but married, and left home after my wife discovered my collection of pornography."

Tony had noticed the absence of a wedding ring on the lady to whom he was speaking. He ventured a guess and asked, "Are you divorced also?"

"I'm afraid so. Hi, I'm Karen Cunningham. Our divorce was final fourteen months and two weeks ago, not that I'm counting or anything. How long for you?"

She had thrown a curve ball that Tony wasn't expecting. Since he wasn't divorced, he could not say for how long, so he carried the conversation elsewhere.

"I'm Tony Taylor. Glad to meet you, Karen. Looks like you are also a Saturday early bird. Think we could have breakfast together next Saturday?"

"Sure!", she laughed. "Then we can do our laundry together. Sounds like a romantic time." By now she had torn off the corner of a newspaper page and was writing on it. "Give me a call this week and we'll set it up."

"Great! I'll bring the soap," Tony joked.

"Try to get Tide, 1998. It was a vintage year for detergents!" Karen fired back. "Looks like my dryer has stopped. Talk to you soon. Bye."

Tony observed the woman who he had just met removing clothes from a dryer. He could not believe that he had a date, well almost a date, with someone so beautiful and witty.

He would later relate the encounter to Mitch, adding "I've never seen a more beautiful woman, and her personality is out of sight. Wonder why I didn't meet her before I married Dee?"

Because, Tony, the woman you just met is a counterfeit of the one-flesh mate that God has given you in Dee. If you were to have given that mailbox store a counterfeit $100 bill, you would have selected the most realistic counterfeit that could be found. Satan is tearing up your home, and doing it very rapidly. Karen is a woman precious to the Lord, but the enemy is using her as a counterfeit. He threw an excellent counterfeit at you and you accepted it. Tony, for the sake of your marriage, throw that telephone number away right now!

Tony looked carefully at the piece of newspaper that Karen had given him. She had written her first name and her phone number on it. Underneath she had drawn a happy face.

"That woman has passed her number before," Tony concluded. He carefully folded his new sinful treasure, put it into his wallet, and went to empty his dryer.

Tony stacked his clean clothes into his car and looked at his watch. It was just after 11:00 A.M. He had hours to kill before going back to the trailer and no place to go. He drove slowly down Broadway, looking at Christmas decorations along the way. He drove all the way to the river and spent a few minutes watching the river boats.

Had Tony known to stop in front of a Christian book store that he passed on Broadway, he might have noticed one of the clerks talking on the telephone. Had he been able to read lips, he might have seen the clerk say "Yes, we have that book on saving a hopeless marriage. I'll put a copy aside for you, Mrs. Taylor."

Tony drove away from the river on Broadway, heading nowhere in particular. In a few minutes, he found himself driving out Lone Oak Road. First he turned right, and then left, went about three blocks and stopped. Ahead one block on the intersecting street was the home of Mr. and Mrs. Anthony Taylor.

"Wonder where a thousand feet would be?" Tony mumbled to himself, recalling the protection order. He had no idea why he had come to his family's neighborhood.

Tony noticed that his wife's car was backed in, a giveaway sign that their son had been the last one to use it. "Wonder what kind of trouble he got into last night without me there to hold the reins on him?" Tony mused. He was once again allowing memories of his own misbehaving at that age to get in the way of a relationship with his son.

It is regrettable that Tony did not know that John had taken the car to work. Two days before, he went out on his own looking for a job. He was hired by a grocery store and had spent Friday evening not getting into trouble, but stocking shelf after shelf of canned goods. His pay would not go for a new computer program or for going out with friends, but would go to his mom to help meet her financial obligations.

There is something else that needs to be reported about young John. Monday evening, after Dee explained in general terms why his dad had moved out, he was in his room for the longest time, and then asked his mom to come in. John's eyes were swollen from crying, and there was a tremble in his voice. His bottom lip quivered as he began to talk.

"Mom," he began, "this is the hardest thing that I have ever had to do. I don't know how to say it, bu -- but, I have one of dad's magazines. I found it in his car and hid it in my room. I came in here a while ago to throw it out. Please don't be mad at me, Mom." By now, John had broken down completely. "I prayed and asked God to forgive me. We have been studying how to hear God in Sunday School, and I know that He forgave me, but I think He told me I had to confess it to you."

Reaching under the mattress where he sat, John produced a manila envelope, carefully sealed with tape. "I just couldn't take a chance," he continued, "on you finding where I threw it and hurting you more. I sealed it up in here so you won't have to look at it," John sobbed. "Please get rid of it. Mom, I am so sorry."

With that, Dee exploded, not with anger, but with tears. She was disappointed, but so proud of her son. He had shown more maturity than his father.

"When I have a son, I don't want him to ever see stuff like that and feel the guilt that I have felt. Mom, I haven't been able to be nice to you or sis because of what I had hidden."

The manila envelope was forgotten for the moment, as a mother and son embraced and sobbed. They had their own moment a short while later in front of the basement furnace. Dee prayed aloud, thanking God that this generational curse had been broken before it reached her grandson, years away from even being born.

Tony sat at the end of his street, thinking he knew what was going on inside his home. Really, he did not have a clue. He did not know about John's confession. He did not know that Dee had spent two hours on the phone with Frances, her prayer partner, and that she was fasting that day for the family. Tony could not see the band of warrior angels that Frances and Dee had prayed all around their home.

He did not know that Dee was about to spend some of her limited funds on books about bondage, spiritual warfare, generational curses, and restoration of a marriage that others would call hopeless. How can that happen? By one spouse taking up the spiritual battle against satan for control of that home.

Whatever Tony expected to see did not take place. He saw no sign of life at all, but there was more life in the heavenly realm than he could have ever imagined. Tony wiped his tears away with the back of his hand, and started the car rolling, once again going nowhere in particular. Not until he started across the bridge into Illinois did he know his destination.

CHAPTER 9

The Lord was preparing to start Dee on a journey that would forever change her life. She would develop a closer relationship with Him than she had ever known. Above all else, she would develop a hunger and thirst for the Bible, God's Holy Word. She would find verses every day that sounded as though they were written by the Lord just for her. She would learn how to claim the promises that God has given in His word.

Just as her son, John, had told her what he was learning, she would learn how to hear from God. She would come to know the power of God, and how much He desires to help His children in every way. Dee was about to become a praying woman, like Frances, who others would think had the ear of God.

Dee was going to learn about spiritual warfare and how to pull down strongholds. She was going to learn how the enemy attacks, and about the ever greater power of God. Although she had been a Christian for most of her life, Dee was about to be awakened to what it is really like to truly walk with the Lord.

By the way, the Lord would be working in her prodigal husband's life during that time. He would bring Tony back to Himself and to his family, but that would be a side benefit to everything else that our Mighty God was doing in Dee's life during that season. Meanwhile, He was going to be her husband for the time that Tony was gone.

God was going to first work in Dee's life, bringing to light all that He would have her change. Along the way, she would ask, in a letter to Tony, "What do I need to change to please you?" The Lord would remind her almost immediately that she had failed to ask Him that same question.

Yes, these were going to be days of very painful hurting for Dee. At times she would be on the verge of giving up on Tony, and "getting on with her life," as everyone seemed to be reminding her to do. Some days she was going to feel that her heart was being ripped from her chest. Each time her spiritual and emotional pain became that acute, she would find her best friend, Jesus, waiting somewhere in the shadows, ever ready to bring her His peace. But first she had to be ready to receive the peace that passes all understanding.

What would have happened if Dee had decided to "get on with her life" and stop praying for Tony? Foremost and never to be forgotten, he might not have ever been delivered from his life of sin, could have died, and gone to hell.

Yes, she could have found another man who wanted her. But God's plan is one man and one woman for a lifetime, so she would not have enjoyed that one-flesh covenant relationship that the Lord had given her and Tony. Even greater, she would be outside of God's will.

How did this spiritual journey start for Dee? Just like every man or woman who has ever faced divorce, she just sensed that something wasn't right. She had that feeling long before she went before the Lord to ask how He saw her marriage.

It might have begun on that Sunday when Tony moved out. The words of her neighbor, Mary Humphries, and all the talk about divorce just did not sit right. The next day when she placed her signature on that first paper in the attorney's office, she had that same feeling. That afternoon, when a policeman stood between her and the husband that had shared her bed only two days before, she knew that something was very wrong.

Incident after incident during that first week of separation confirmed the thought that she was making a mistake. She had spent practically no time in prayer that week. Finally on Friday evening, she called Frances. That was the first time her prayer partner knew they had separated.

"Honey," Frances had reassured her, "you and Tony are going through God's refining fire to make you pure. The Lord loves both of you too much, and has too much for you to do, to leave either of you unclean vessels."

Frances had sensed on that preceding Sunday that Tony had sin in his life. Not until Dee had shared about finding the pornography and the females' phone numbers, did Frances share any of what the Lord had revealed to her.

"You said that God is refining both of us," Dee clarified. "Tony is the one with the sexual addiction. God needs to work on him, not me."

Frances tactfully and prayerfully took Dee through a spiritual inventory. Dee became aware of several areas where the Lord would have her to change, not small things such as leaving dirty dishes in the sink, but a slack prayer life and a critical spirit.

By the conclusion of that lengthy call, Dee had made progress. She had confessed several things to her prayer partner, but the one area of Dee's life that she had never shared with anyone remained closed.

Saturday, Dee drove downtown to the book store and purchased the first books that would become quite a library. That afternoon, she read book after book that seemed written just about Tony and his stronghold of sexual addiction. She did encounter two references to the secret area of her life, but quickly skipped over them. She was too busy finding out what was wrong with Tony to open up her own hidden hurts.

In church on the following Sunday, Dee went to the altar during prayer time. Pastor Scott Wilson, sitting on the platform, saw her responding. On the previous Sunday, the Lord had given him a word of knowledge that Dee's husband was involved with pornography. He had noticed Tony sitting motionless during his entire sermon. Pastor Wilson had also noted the conviction that Tony had been under when he "drew the net," inviting people to respond to the claims of Christ on their life. Tony had actually made false starts into the aisle, drawing quickly back into the pew.

This Sunday, Pastor Wilson met Dee at the altar and prayed with her. "I only told him that I was seeking prayer for my marriage," she later shared with Frances. "And he prayed as though he knew every detail, even about the sexual addiction and pornography."

On that Sunday morning, although she knew very little about how she would do it, Dee pledged to God that she would not divorce Tony. Instead, she would fast and pray that his strongholds might be torn down. "Everyone will think I am crazy, but I refuse to deliver my family over to the enemy by bringing us through a divorce!", she confided in Pastor Wilson. "I can't keep my husband out of hell, but I can sure pray to the One who can."

Pastor Scott Wilson did have a sensitive spirit for men addicted to pornography. He and his wife, Samantha, talked about it often. Her dad was the pastor of a growing church up in Indiana. He had entered the ministry later in life, after a successful career as an accountant.

Samantha's dad had been involved in pornography for years, when she was a youngster and into her teen years. He had followed his fantasies, as most sexual addicts do. He needed more and more to satisfy himself, and eventually divorced his wife, Julie. Sam and Julie had a rough time, until Tom Grant was gloriously called back to the Lord, and later to pastoral ministries. They had helped scores of couples save their marriages through the years.

It was difficult to imagine that the pastor who was now touching so many lives, had years ago, been so deeply involved in online pornography and chat rooms. His screen name, "CHICAGOMAN," was known around the world as a funny, but sin-sick man. Scott and Samantha Wilson had prayed against that spirit, breaking a generational curse that could have been passed on to her. Having been a part of this curse with his wife, Pastor Wilson now had a kind spirit for men caught in that net of satan.

Dee was wise in covering her husband's nakedness. On that Sunday, and for many Sundays afterward, she had many opportunities to disclose the story about pornography to many people asking about Tony. Her standard answer became, "I am praying for him. Will you also?"

Sister Wilson, Pastor Wilson's wife, caught up with Dee after church. Her one-flesh relationship with her husband allowed her to sense what was happening at the altar during that service. She noticed how intense her husband had been while he prayed for Dee. She noted his look of concern while Dee spoke to him. Those indicators, combined with the absence of Tony, showed her that she had to talk to Dee.

"Hi, Dee, I'm Samatha Wilson, Pastor Wilson's helpmate. I've known who you are, but have not had the opportunity to meet you since we arrived."

Dee's spirits were boosted by a pastor's wife singling her out. This came on a day when Dee needed to be encouraged in a very serious way.

"I'm glad to meet you. How do you like Paducah so far?"

"This is going to be the best place the Lord has ever taken us to minister. We are really excited to be here."

Dee appreciated the way that Samantha had used the term

"us" in describing ministry. This was a pastor's wife who co-ministered with her husband.

"I would love to get to know you," Samantha said. "We would love to have you come over for dinner some night this week. Are you free Tuesday or Thursday night?"

Pastor Wilson had been captured by a church board member on the other side of the foyer. He observed his wife talking to a smiling and happy Dee, and silently thanked God for the sensitive co-laborer and one-flesh mate with which he had been blessed. The "un-hun's" he gave to the board member, reporting on some imagined wrong, were automatic.

He was talking with the Lord about Dee and Tony Taylor. Just as the churchman completed his monologue, Pastor Scott saw his wife and Dee embrace. Samantha had exercised her God-given gift of encouragement once again. "I just thank the Lord for you," he said aloud.

"Thanks, Pastor," the board member replied. "I thought you would want to know all about it." With that, he walked away, pleased that the associate pastor had listened to his complaint.

On the way home, Dee shared with her two children that the Lord had told her to pray for her prodigal husband.

"Does that mean Daddy will be home real soon?" an excited Deborah asked, leaning over the front seat.

"Not quite, stupid!" her brother answered. "It means that God will do what He wants with Dad, when He wants to do it. Mom, I want to pray for Dad also."

How could Dee correct a son for calling his sister "stupid?", when he had followed the inappropriate comment with such a statement.

"Me too, Mommy, me too!" Deborah joined in. "I want to pray for Daddy too. Look, there's the state policeman that stopped Daddy last Sunday. I want to wave at him."

Had it only been a week since Tony had been in church with them? It seemed like a lifetime. During that brief time, Dee's emotions had been all over the chart. She had been mad, and then sad; hopeless, and then encouraged; ashamed, and then afraid. Really, it did not matter what Dee was feeling, for her Lord had not changed one bit since Tony walked out that door seven days before. He is the lover of lost sheep and will not give up on them until they come back into the fold. Dee would be happiest when she stood with the Lord for Tony's restoration.

"Stop it, jerk!" John screamed at his sister. "You're making a fool out of yourself." Deborah was vigorously waving at the gray Kentucky Highway Patrol car that was backed in alongside the road.

"John, don't talk to your sister that way. What's wrong with you, anyway? You were raised better than that!"

Yes, he had been raised to behave better than that, but when a father suddenly kicks out all the stops and goes to live the selfish life that he desires, even the best of children are adversely affected. If the most severe behavior problem that her son would demonstrate was to yell at his sister, Dee would be very fortunate indeed. Dee had read the studies that demonstrate the disadvantage that divorcing parents bring to their children. They have been documented to have increased drug problems, truancy, and teen pregnancy. But there are a few areas where these children show decreases: in grades, ability to make their own marriages work, and ability to keep a job.

"Look, Mommy, look!" an excited Deborah was screaming. Although it was so quick that Dee missed it, her daughter didn't. In response to a little girl's excited wave, the trooper had flipped on his patrol car's lights for a split second. Not until the vehicle had passed, did Trooper Tremonte recognize that car. In response to complaints, he had been assigned to run radar again that Sunday in the same location as the previous week.

Bud Tremonte had been a police officer for many years, first in Michigan, and now in Kentucky. He could "read" drivers. The operator of that vehicle, with both hands gripping the wheel and bearing a stern expression, appeared to him to be someone with troubles. The absence of the man he had stopped the week before, combined with the driver's demeanor, would have been enough to let him know what was happening. Far greater, the Holy Spirit of God convicted Bud to pray for that family.

"Lord, touch them, regardless of what is going on. May Your spirit convict and bring repentance to that home. Father, please help them avoid all that Christine and I put our girls through, I humbly ask in Jesus' name, Amen." The steady beep of his radar machine and flashing digits brought Bud back from the heavenlies to a rural road in Kentucky. He saw the Taylor car off in the distance and quickly prayed, *"Lord, touch that man and bring him to his senses,"* as he pulled onto the road for another traffic stop.

Although Trooper Tremonte would not have recognized the vehicle, he might have recognized the driver, had he been in that location earlier Sunday morning. Just as the sun was coming up, Tony Taylor was making his way to the small trailer in West Paducah that he had been calling home. That was all about to change.

Tony had come back across the bridge Saturday afternoon. He had stopped at a pay phone. Pulling the corner of a newspaper page from his wallet, he called Karen Cunningham, whom he had met at the laundromat. She had been as witty on the phone as she had been in person. Karen and Tony had talked and laughed on the phone for the longest time. He accepted her invitation to dinner without hesitation. As only a prodigal spouse is able to do, he had placed his wife and two precious children totally out of his mind for the moment. But the Lord would not allow Tony to forget those who loved him.

Tony had been on his way to the trailer to move out. After having known Karen for only one day (and night), he had readily accepted her offer to rent him a room in her home. Tony Taylor, the sex addict, was falling deeper and deeper into sin. "Lord, touch that man and bring him to his senses."

CHAPTER 10

Dee had been correct when she told her neighbor, "This isn't going to be much of a Christmas." She went through all the motions with her two children, but there was something missing. It was her husband. Every time she went to church, she only observed couples. More than once, she had awakened in the morning and extended her arm to the other side of the bed. Instead of touching Tony's shoulder, her hand would rest on a bed so empty that even the pillow had been taken away.

Although she was experiencing an empty Christmas, she was being blessed by a more Christ-centered Christmas than she had ever imagined possible. The kids were hurting, but they also appreciated their Christmas activities more than ever.

During the Christmas season, Dee canceled her divorce and had the Protection Order vacated. These were both accomplished by a less-than-pleased Attorney Godalson. He could not understand the "silliness" of hearing from God to hang on to a marriage. After several less than pleasant phone calls, and several releases exchanged by mail, the divorce of Tony and Dee had officially been canceled.

It appeared that Dee had lost most of the retainer that she had paid to her attorney. He had promised her an itemization of charges, but went on to explain that his time had been "significant" in stopping the divorce.

It was amazing how often some friend felt responsible to report Tony's activities to Dee. He continued to receive his mail at the mail center box. After the divorce was canceled, she mailed Tony a note, asking him to call her. Two days later, right before Christmas, Tony called the phone number he knew so well. He could not imagine what Dee wanted. Tony had been at a holiday party given by a friend, just before that 9:00 P.M. call.

Dee had given up hope that Tony would call that day. She was lying in bed, reading her Bible and talking to the Lord, asking for His help in purchasing gifts for her family. She barely had enough to pay bills and buy food. Both children had gone to sleep early, and this was her time to be with the Lord. Her devotion time was interrupted by the ringing of the phone.

"Hello."

"What do you want?" Tony replied sternly.

"Tony, it's good to hear your voice! How are you?"

"How do you think I am? You had the police put me out of my own house! You messed up all our charge accounts! I don't have enough money to live on, and you told that preacher to preach at me! I have been sleeping in my car and not eating! Now, how do you think I am?"

"Tony, I'm so sorry. Please forgive me . I was just blinded. Can't you see, satan wants to destroy our family, and he began with you. Please, please forgive me for my part."

"Please forgive me for my part?", Tony squealed back at his wife. "I will never forgive you because you almost killed me. Now why did I have to call you? Wanna put me in jail or sumthunn?"

"This is not my husband," Dee thought. She then ventured out on thin ice. "Tony, have you been drinking?"

"I sure have, and looking at my books at the same time. What are you gonna do? Call the law? Woman, you are history. I found someone else, a real woman who knows how to have a good time. Thanks for divorcing me. Best thing that ever happened to me! By the way, her name is Karen Cunningham. Look her up in the phone book and maybe she can tell you how to be a real woman. How soon is our divorce final? I want to get married to a real woman!"

The background noise stopped and five seconds later Dee was listening to a dial tone. Her husband had once again disappeared into the cold December night. Dee was devastated. The call from Tony had not ended as she had envisioned.

At first, Dee began to cry. Then she reached for the phone to call Frances, who always retired early. She hung up the phone and began to scream at satan to leave her husband alone. She was mad! No, not at her husband, nor at the other woman, but at the devil, who was causing all this.

Fearing that her yelling at satan would awaken her children, Dee grabbed her heavy robe and her Bible. She headed for the basement stairs and descended into that cold tomb. She found her way to the far end where the furnace was located. She sat down on the cement floor. Her screams and sobs were drowned out by the noisy old furnace.

Dee read scripture; she prayed; she shouted at the enemy and then she would start all over. For the first time that night, Dee got down to serious business in breaking the strongholds that were binding her husband.

Dee could not say why she went to the furnace room that night, but it soon became her prayer closet. The gates of hell must have trembled each time that woman, armed only with the precious Word of God, descended those stairs.

There was something special about the flame that illuminated Dee's private prayer closet. Foremost it reminded her of Jesus, the Light of the World. The warmth it produced reminded her of the comforting presence of God's Holy Spirit. Peering inside the open furnace reminded of her of hell's eternal fire and of the urgency to pray for Tony.

Every man or woman who has taken a stand with God for

restoration of his or her marriage has experienced the equivalent of the call Dee received that night. The enemy delights in confirming to the children of the King that their greatest fear has come true. To Dee, it was hearing that her husband was involved with someone else, and that he was drinking for the first time in his life. To another, it might be hearing that their spouse is about to make a futile attempt to legalize adultery by entering into a non-covenant relationship (and that IS NOT a marriage!). To someone else praying for restoration of their marriage, their most feared call might be news that a child is expected from a sinful affair. To yet another, it might be news that their absent spouse is moving a great distance away.

Can't you see that satan will use whatever is most likely to defeat a stander? It does not matter what is heard. It does matter how that news is handled. Consider Dee's options. She had just learned the name of the other woman. How easy it might have been to call her up or go confront her in person. She also could have gone looking for Tony or confront him at work the next day.

Congratulations, Sister Dee. You handled that opposition in a way that pleased the Lord and did not bring discredit to Him. And He is about to reward you.

About an hour later, Dee was still in her prayer closet, praying, binding, and reading her Bible. She found herself humming a tune and repeating words that could have been a chorus. Then she realized the Lord was giving her a simple song. She hurriedly found a pen and began to write in the back of her Bible:

> *Lord, grant it in Your perfect time,*
> *I will again be his and he'll be mine.*
> *I look to no one else, but to You alone,*
> *You sent Your son for my sins to atone.*
> *It matters not what others might say,*

For my covenant spouse I'll always pray.
Satan's on notice to take no more ground,
I've called God's warrior angels all around.
There's coming a day of precious holy victory
When Your face my dear prodigal shall see.
Lord, grant it in Your perfect time
I will again be his and he'll be mine.

Dee sang her "song" over and over, each time singing louder. Finally, she thanked the Lord for comforting her and blessing her with a song. She forgave Tony and asked the Lord to protect him. Then she went up the stairs, climbed into bed and enjoyed the best night's sleep she had experienced in two weeks.

CHAPTER 11

Although Dee's faith was growing by leaps and bounds, she was worried. The following day was Christmas Eve and she was broke. She had purchased only nickel and dime gifts for her son and daughter. Dee had put up only minimal decorations inside the home and none on the outside.

Since having dinner with her pastor two weeks before, the Wilsons quickly become close friends. Samantha called Dee almost daily to pray with her. Dee really appreciated that couple and had shared several things with them that she had never told anyone else. But she did not disclose her deepest secret, safely tucked away for years, covered by scar tissue in her heart.

On that day of financial panic, Dee thought about calling the parsonage and asking for help with Christmas for her children. Samantha had been instantly drawn to Deborah. She had even shared how her own father had left her and her mom for a while, how God brought him back, and how he ended up becoming a preacher.

Dee thought that maybe Sam could take Deborah Christmas shopping. That would resolve part of her problem. Just as Dee started to make that phone call, she seemed to hear the Lord say, "Tell your need to Me, not to other people. I will answer in such a way that you will know it to be My miracle." Dee hung up the phone and began to pray for the means to provide for her children's Christmas.

When the doorbell rang that afternoon, she was certain the Lord had sent an angel with the answer to her Christmas prayer. Peeking out, Dee saw Samantha Wilson standing beside a huge basket of groceries.

"Oh, no!", she thought. "Not that!" Her first impulse was

to run and hide in her prayer closet that doubled as a furnace room. Last year, she and Tony had delivered Christmas baskets, and now she was receiving one. So much had changed so quickly. Dee was angry, not at Tony, but at satan, for trying to tear up her family.

The pastor's wife explained that the Taylor name had been listed as "Anonymous" on the list of those receiving baskets, so that no one would know she received help, apart from the Wilsons.

"We want Tony to be able to hold his head high at church, just as soon as he repents and makes things right with the Lord," Samantha declared wisely.

Dee had walked Samantha to her car, when a second vehicle stopped in front of the Taylors. As soon as she recognized it, her heart skipped a beat. "Sam, please wait," she pleaded, "that's the messenger from the attorney's office. He was angry that I stopped the divorce. What am I going to do if he wants more money?"

The driver greeted Dee and handed her an envelope that did indeed bear the return address of that law firm. Samantha must have been praying as Dee hurriedly tore open the envelope. She found a letterhead from the attorney that displayed not a typed, formal letter, but a handwritten note:

"Mrs. Taylor,

Perhaps I've been a crusty old divorce attorney for too many years, but your desire to rebuild your marriage has touched me. My wife related last evening of someone in her church who is attempting to accomplish the same thing. Her explanation made sense to me.

Enclosed please find a refund of your unused retainer. I am asking my secretary to have it delivered to you today, in case you need holiday money. Merry Christmas!"

Underneath was the scribbled signature of J. William Godalson. A check had been folded inside the letter.

With tears in her eyes, Dee looked at the check for the first time. It was for $3,500! Anyone driving by just then must have wondered what was happening, with two women literally jumping in the air with joy.

On Christmas morning, there were presents under the Taylor's tree. The bills had been paid and Dee had reopened a savings account on Christmas Eve. The Lord had provided.

"If the Lord can restore a savings account," she had testified to Frances, "then having our marriage restored is a done deal!"

Dee, John, and Deborah had Christmas dinner with the pastor, as did Frances. We don't know what Tony was doing at about 1:00 P.M. that day, but heaven was being bombarded with prayers from all around that dinner table, thanking God for sending His son, and asking Him to touch Tony.

Samantha Wilson had invited that same group of people back to their home on New Year's Eve. She had said that "a couple other people" were coming. Although she did not know it, Dee was in for a real blessing.

When Dee and her children arrived that night, they pulled in behind a car bearing a license plate from Indiana. That was not all that unusual since Paducah is located so close to Indiana, so she gave it no thought. Once inside, Samantha introduced her arriving guests as her dad and mom, Reverend and Mrs. Tom Grant, also known by some as "CHICAGOMAN." That night, as the new year was arriving, Dee was standing in a circle with two pastors and their wives, her children, and her prayer partner, all praying for the Lord to touch Tony in the new year.

Pastor Grant had symbolically turned his hands down, releasing anything of the flesh that was being done to bring Tony home.

After a beautiful evening of fellowship, Dee and her kids started for home. "Watch out for New Year's Eve drunk drivers!", Pastor Wilson called out the door to Dee. He was not aware that he was reminding Dee to watch out for her own husband.

That holiday night, Tony had been arrested for the first time in his life. He had been stopped at a DUI checkpoint, set up by the Sheriff's Office. Tony had spent the night in jail, too ashamed to call Dee, and assuming she had no bail money. After his initial court appearance that next morning, Tony pled not guilty and was released pending trial.

That night in jail had been a sobering experience for Tony, not only as time removed the alcohol from his system, but also by what he had witnessed. Someone in his holding cell had a pornographic magazine. For the first time in his life, he was sickened by what he was hearing verbalized about the women in that magazine.

The Lord did not break open that cell, as He did for Paul and Silas. But He was reaching down into that filthy cell at midnight and calling for one of His lost sheep to repent.

Tony, you've made a mess of your life. How much more will it take for the Lord to get your attention? Your wife might not be the richest woman in Paducah, but she is being blessed by new friendships and a close walk with Jesus Christ. Your life continues to unravel. Prodigal, come home, to a waiting family and to a waiting Lord.

CHAPTER 12

January saw Dee growing closer to the Lord each day. During that month, she had some phone contact with Tony. He was furious when he found that she had canceled the divorce action. Tony had threatened to file if Dee did not. There was not a single phone call when Dee did not invite Tony to come home.

One time he called her with a strange request. "I know you are really into the religion thing now, so how about praying for a little problem that I have?"

"I am always honored to pray for my husband." Dee was wise not to press for details, which Tony volunteered in the next breath.

"I have a little legal thing. It's really a misunderstanding. I'm not guilty or anything, but prayer never hurts, right?"

"You are right, Tony. I will be praying for you until you come home."

"Don't do that 'coming home' drill on me any more. I am never coming home. Period! What part of 'never' don't you understand? I made a mistake in calling you, sorry!" Again she experienced one of those abrupt endings that Tony often gave the call to his wife.

"That's plain old Holy Spirit conviction," Frances had later explained to her. "There is so much of the Holy Spirit being demonstrated through your voice that sinful Tony can't stand it. You keep it up dear, just keep it up. The Lord is moving!"

One cold day in February, Dee drove to her favorite bookstore downtown, in search of a new study book that would help her as she prayed for restoration of her family. One of the owners saw her coming in the door, and pulled a note out of the cash register.

"Hi, welcome in out of the winter. I'm sorry that I didn't remember your name, but a lady came in last week searching for some of the same books that you have bought. She said that she is 'standing' for the restoration of her marriage. You and she are the only two people who have ever come in looking for restoration books. Most people want divorce adjustment books."

"That customer said that she did not know anyone else in Paducah was standing for their marriage. I took down her name and number and promised to give it you the next time you were in. Here it is."

Dee was thrilled. Had snow not started to fall, she would have stopped at a pay phone to call Sylvia Pierce. It was fortunate that she did not stop because they talked for almost three hours and she would have frozen to death. Only someone who has been at the bottom looking up to God, and discovered someone else right in the same circumstances, can appreciate what that call meant to Dee. Sylvia would soon join the ranks of Frances and the Wilsons, praying for the restoration of Tony, and of the marriage, confident that God would do both.

Dee did not know there were ministries that worked with spouses, standing alone with God, and praying for restoration of their marriage. Sylvia introduced her to two such organizations, half a continent apart. One was in Oklahoma and the other was in Florida.

Dee contacted both and began to order material. It wasn't long before her mailbox brought not attorney letters, but newsletters, books, tapes, and other gems of hope.

The ministry in Oklahoma had an upcoming conference on July 4th weekend. Although it looked impossible due to finances, Dee began to ask the Lord to make a way for her to attend.

Sylvia had offered to share a hotel room with her, and the Wilsons has offered to keep Deborah for the weekend. The parents of a church friend of John's had given their permission for John to spend the weekend with them.

Both children were excited about the possibility of staying with others. Dee sensed this was due to the fact that their dad never saw them, apart from a fast food meal once every two weeks. He continued to live with Karen and was hesitant to take his children there, for which Dee was thankful. She had been devastated enough when Deborah, in the innocence of her childhood, had told about meeting Karen at one of their hamburger meals. Dee could not imagine having her children in that woman's home. Karen had stolen her husband, and that was enough.

Dee could have told you, almost to the cent, how much it would take for her to go to Oklahoma. Although the expenses were more than reasonable, to her they looked impossible.

As spring approached, there was an incident that gave her renewed hope. Unfortunately, it involved the death of Tony's best friend from church.

"Tony," Dee exclaimed to her husband one spring morning, after calling him at the shop. "Barney's had a heart attack and is being taken to Baptist Hospital. Can you take your lunch hour and run up the street to the hospital to pray with Carole?" In the past, "Preacher Man's" employer had been extremely co-operative in allowing him to adjust his schedule at times like this.

"It sounds serious," Dee pleaded. "They were doing CPR when he was brought out of the house."

"Uhhh," Tony stalled for time, "we're in the middle of a mess here right now and I couldn't get away for anything." In truth, Tony thought that he might have forgotten how to pray.

Barney did go on to be with the Lord that day. His funeral was scheduled for Saturday morning at the church. Dee attended, and sat down in the same pew where she sat three times a week. As she always did, each time she came to church, she began to pray for Tony.

Just as Pastor Wilson stood up to open the service, Dee felt a nudge on her shoulder, and looked around to see Tony motioning her to slide over. She had no idea why he was there, but could see that he was visibly shaken. Was it because he was back in church, or was it because his best friend, one year younger than him, had gone on to glory?

Tony was not uneducated in the things of Christ, although he had chosen to turn his back on them. Tony knew that if his physical body were lying there, his soul would be condemned to hell. That was a more sobering thought than his night in jail had been.

Although this was a funeral service, Pastor Scott Wilson preached as though he was talking to a dying man, for indeed he was. He had noticed Tony slipping in, and could not seem to keep his attention on that bereaved family. He knew that each of them was right with the Lord and that Tony was not. Had any of that church family known all of the circumstances, they would have asked the preacher to bring a message that might convict Tony of his wrongdoing.

Silently Dee was thanking the Lord for having her husband sit in church with her. Midway through the service, Dee noticed that Tony's hand nearest her was shaking. "Lord, should I?" she silently prayed. Then she reached over and took Tony's hand, anticipating that he would pull away, or possibly even leave the funeral. Instead, he did nothing. Dee could not imagine how a man could remain as motionless as Tony did.

As the benediction was being said, Tony squeezed Dee's hand so hard that it almost hurt. Just as Pastor Wilson sat down, and as the funeral directors were coming forward to dismiss the service, Tony quickly released his wife's hand, and exited without saying a word.

There was a battle between right and wrong, between darkness and light, that was taking place within Tony Taylor. The intensity of that struggle cannot be imagined by anyone who has not experienced it. Every prodigal spouse who has ever walked the rocky and often winding path back to a praying family could describe that raging war, if only there were words.

On one hand, we want so badly to do what we know is right, that is to go home. On the other, we are being pressured to keep going the opposite direction. That pressure comes from selfish desire, pride, shame, lust, and yes, from that ever-present other person. The Lord knows what it will take to bring us home. Satan only thinks he knows what it will take to keep us away. Thus, the battle rages. It is not a simple childish tug of war, with one side gaining and then losing ground. The battle rages with all the force and intensity of a bolt of electricity dancing back and forth between two rods.

That battle rages until one of two events takes place. If the one praying and fasting for that prodigal ceases to fight the spiritual battle, the enemy shuts down his attack, because he has won. How much greater the results if that one fighting the battle continues to intensify their attack with spiritual warfare, burning away every conductor that has been set in place to arrest that charge, until God can deliver the power to bring conviction and repentance to another prodigal. That is when Prodigals Do Come Home! To God be the glory.

All across America and around the world are thousands, if not millions, of Dee Taylors who have declared, "Devil, enough is enough! I've drawn the line, and it is just beyond my marriage and my family. Evil one, you are defeated in the mighty name of Jesus and His blood shed for me. You go back to hell where you came from and where you belong! Thank you, Father God, for The Power. By faith, I am claiming my marriage as healed. Amen and Amen."

Tony Taylor had walked out of the funeral service at his church, with no particular place to go. He could not go back to Karen's where he was living, yet mistakenly thought that he could not go home to Dee. Tony drove and drove. As if he had no control over it, his car headed across that bridge.

That evening, on the drive back across the river into Kentucky, Tony was feeling guilty. He thought about where he had just been, he also thought about what he had heard Pastor Wilson share earlier that day: "Barney wasn't a perfect man, but he was a forgiven man. Just as He did for Barney, God can forgive you for anything that you have done. The Lord only asks that you confess and repent, turn away from whatever it might be that has you into sin."

For some strange reason, Tony thought about Calvin and that first magazine. For the first time, his thoughts conjured up the term "sexual addiction" as he looked back on a lifetime of pornography and unfaithfulness. He considered how many times he had entertained inappropriate thoughts about a female, even in church. "No wonder I'm messed up," Tony said aloud. I have been stuffing so much junk for all these years. I think I'll change." Fifteen minutes later, he pulled in Karen's driveway.

As often happens when a prodigal mate feels they have drawn too close to their praying spouse, Tony drew back. He even missed burger night that next week, making a son furious and breaking the heart of a ten year old daughter, who sat waiting for him by the door, refusing to believe that her daddy would not show up.

Dee did not recall everything that she had prayed down by the furnace, and she had not yet begun to keep a journal, recording all that the Lord was showing her. Had she been journaling, Dee would have recalled that during one especially difficult evening (Yes, many are difficult, even for strong standers) she had asked the Lord if she could only sit in church with Tony, holding his hand, as a sign that the Lord was moving. On this very day, that had taken place.

CHAPTER 13

With Easter approaching, Dee just "knew" that Resurrection Day would be the day of resurrection for her marriage. God had not told Dee this, she just "knew" it. You see, that revelation was not from the spirit of God, but from the spirit of Dee. It could have even been from an evil spirit, sent to deceive and discourage Dee. When Easter came, with no Tony, Dee was devastated, and considered giving up.

Her hopes went up a week later when Tony called her one evening. "I've broken up with Karen and moved back in with Mitch, a friend of mine from work," Tony announced with anger in his voice. "I hope you're happy because you broke us up!"

Dee had done not a thing to end that relationship, but the Lord certainly had, in response to the faithful prayers of a hurting wife.

"Tony, I have never even met or talked to that woman."

"It doesn't matter," he fired back with indignation. "All of your praying messed up the good life that we could have had together. Thanks for nothing."

Although he concluded the call in typical Tony style, by slamming down the phone, this time it did not matter! Tony was on the way home! Praise God, the other woman was out of the picture. Dee was thrilled! She had heard enough from Tony about the living conditions at Mitch's to know that she had more praying to do.

By this time, Frances was meeting weekly with both Dee and Sylvia. The trio was praying for the restoration of all marriages, especially the two represented there. Sylvia was receiving tapes from the ministry in Florida that were recorded at a local stander's Bible study. They never knew when those tapes were coming, but each time a new one arrived, the trio would get together to listen, discuss what they had heard, and then pray together. These were indeed faith-building sessions.

On one tape, the teacher had mentioned something about men and women who had been abused as children, either sexually or physically. She shared scriptures that promised healing for their wounded hearts. The teacher also made a comment about how prevalent abuse was, and how the victims suffered. She had referred to old abuse as "excess baggage" that the stander needed to deal with. "If you were a victim and have been stuffing it for years, bring it before the Lord. We don't want anything to stand in the way of the Lord bringing your spouse home," she added. As was her teaching style, the speaker was off to another verse and another topic, attempting to get as much as possible on that sixty minute tape.

Dee must have felt like Tony had back on the Advent Sunday when he heard Pastor Wilson tear into pornography. Although Dee was sitting at her own kitchen table, she was embarrassed. During the past months, she had confided in her two friends and prayer partners about everything, except "that."

The teacher prayed one of her long and very powerful prayers at the end of that tape. One of that trio offered a "wow," and they began to talk about the lesson just taught.

Sylvia's eyes had filled with tears. When she started to speak, she was choked up as well.

"I need. . .I need to get rid of something that I have been carrying inside for over thirty years. No one knows this but me and him, but I was abused when I was six years old." Sylvia went on to share details that need not be repeated here. It was obvious that her wound had been festering for over a quarter of a century.

As often happens, the sincere confession of someone else in the body of Christ opens the way and makes it easier for others to deal with their sin issues. That was happening on this day. As soon as Sylvia was finished, Dee told her story of sexual abuse. It was the first time that she had even as much as acknowledged that it happened. She felt as though a huge weight had been lifted off of her heart with each word she shared in confidence with the Lord, and with her two friends.

Frances had her eyes closed while Dee was confessing. She was talking to her Jesus about how she could best minister to two wounded women.

All three women were weeping. Had we been able to see what was happening in the heavenlies, it is possible that we would have seen our Lord Jesus standing next to that table, with His arms around all three women. He had come to that table to comfort and to heal.

After Dee had finished sharing, Frances spoke. "I won't give details or names, but the Lord has led several abused women into my life down through the years. I say this with no pride, but with praise to the Lord, but He has given me the ability to minister to women who have been abused. My eyesight is so bad that I can't read them now, but I have several books that will help you. Of course, The Book is going to help most of all," Frances chuckled one of her typical chuckles, breaking the tension.

Dee and Sylvia discovered that each of their abuse incidents had much in common. The abusers were both dead now. Both had been family members. No one had ever been told of the incident. Both had been rewarded by the abuser not to tell, and threatened if they ever did. Neither of their prodigal husbands had a clue what had happened. Both had carried the thought for years and years that the abuse had been their fault. Both women could trace a lifetime of feeling inferior because of the incident. Both had experienced flashbacks of the incident while with their husbands. Both felt extremely dirty. Neither had ever thought that the Lord could forgive them, even though they had done nothing wrong. Both felt great release by dealing with their secret.

The trio had an especially powerful time of prayer that day. "It is almost as if the Lord is standing right here with us," one had remarked. If only she knew.

Frances did provide books for the other two women, but those details would never be discussed again. From that day forward, either could utter the word "abuse" without cringing.

Why had the Holy Spirit orchestrated that tape, with that topic, on that day? Foremost He loved those two devoted women so much that He wanted to erase and forgive that area of hurt. The Lord was also preparing them to be the wives that their restored husbands would need and deserve. Thirdly, God would place other victims of sexual abuse in their paths down through the years. Once healed, they would be able to share that healing with others.

As their small group was breaking up, Dee joked, "Now that stuff is out of the way, I sure hope the Lord finds time to work on my Tulsa trip. I want to go so badly." She was not begging, but sharing her heart's desire with two sisters who now knew everything about her that there was to know. Watching her friends depart, Dee felt cleaner than she had ever felt before.

Either of those other two women could have offered to sponsor Dee's trip. Both listened to the Holy Spirit for everything they did. For some strange reason, neither felt led to help get Dee to her conference.

CHAPTER 14

With Karen out of the picture, and Dee having dealt with every (yes, every) area of her life that the Lord had brought to mind, she just knew that Tony was on the way home. She was also confident that on July 4th, she would not be watching Paducah's fireworks down on the river. The Lord would have her in Tulsa! She envisioned what it must be like to be in a conference with hundreds of other people who were also standing for their marriage to be restored on the solid rock of Jesus Christ. Dee was especially looking forward to hearing the testimonies of restored marriages.

The enemy knew exactly when to pull out his big gun, thinking that he was moving in for the kill of that marriage. Deborah came running in from burger night with her dad a week later to share what she thought was good news.

"Daddy is living in a new, big house that is really nice. There is a woman there named Amy and she is rich! Look, she gave me five dollars," Deborah concluded with excitement ringing in her voice.

"Way to go, big mouth," John interrupted, "just shut up will you?"

This time Dee did not correct her son's talk to his sister.

"Mom," John consoled, "Dad has moved in with another woman. Yes, she is rich. I love my dad, but why does she want to live with a mechanic who is supposed to be home with his family? People are squirrelly, sometimes. I just don't understand it."

"It's no use. He will never change," Dee wailed. "He has a sexual addiction that the Lord isn't touching. O God, O God please show me what to do!"

"What's a sexel dixon?" young Deborah inquired.

"It's what people get who read the wrong books and watch bad things on TV," her sixteen year old brother responded.

"I never want to catch it then," she replied. "Did Daddy leave us because of those books he hid in his closet?"

"How do you know about that?" a stunned Dee asked.

"I ran in from playing to get a drink and I saw him in the gun box. He was smiling and I saw a really bad picture that I can't tell you about."

Dee was stunned as if she had just been hit with a club.

Nothing could have been more devastating than to hear that her ten year old daughter had been even remotely exposed to her husband's pornography. That was it! She was giving up praying for her marriage. Tony could, and would go to hell, and that was what he deserved. At least that is what Dee shared with Sylvia, Frances, and Samantha.

Dee did not really call all three of the women who were praying with her to ask them for prayer. If she were giving up, she did not need their permission. She was doing exactly what she had heard not to do so many times on those tapes: taking a survey. She had asked three women what they thought about giving up, but she had not asked the Lord. That is exactly what three sisters in the Lord reminded her that afternoon.

Although it was a warm spring day, Dee headed down to her prayer closet in the furnace room and sought the Lord. He gave her verse after verse to reassure her that she was to be praying for Tony. Dee had been so blessed that she came up those basement stairs two at a time. She was now sure the Lord was going to open the doors for her to go to Oklahoma.

That day, the Lord had revealed yet another area of her life where change was needed. She had gone before the Lord with her foremost concern being her daughter. The Lord had reminded her of how often she had been saying "No" to Deborah and John, when they wanted some little outing with their Mom. John, at 16, did have frequent access to her car, but Deborah's needs had been placed behind her stand and her prayer partners.

That evening, both of her children looked shocked when Dee asked if they would like to go out to dinner. Apparently John made the decision on where to go for they ended up at one of those famous west Kentucky Bar-B-Que places, a real treat for anyone.

After they ate, Deborah asked if they could stop at "some places" and pulled a handwritten list from her pocket. The child's needs were being overlooked by her mom, busy standing for her marriage. Deborah had made a list of what they could do together now and not "after Daddy comes home."

That evening was spent doing what was important to a ten year old: Returning an overdue library book, going to the drug store for a new hair brush, and window shopping at the Paducah Mall. Deborah wanted to look at windows with dresses for girls and puppies at the pet store.

"I won't ask you to buy me anything," little Deborah explained as Dee parked the car. "I know we don't have much money until after Daddy comes home."

The comments about not asking for anything had stung Dee, as did Deborah's "after daddy comes home." What would Dee have said if she had given up on Tony that afternoon?

Dee did not know why a sixteen year old boy would welcome going to the mall with his mom and little sister, until she noticed him slicking down his hair, so that he would look good for the teen-age girls.

Dee's thoughts went back to John's confession about pornography. "One of these little girls will be thanking God in a few years that the generational curse of Tony's had not been passed on," she thought, observing her son trying to act "hot" for a pack of giggling girls.

That special night ended with ice cream. Dee had no idea how much mother/daughter chat Deborah had stored up, until she began talking. For the first time in many weeks, she said prayers individually with each of her children, and tucked them in. Those prayers included binding the spirit of divorce that had been loosed on her family.

Late that night, when Dee was doing her devotions, she had to confess to the Lord that she had almost failed her children.

"Lord, they lost their dad, and I also walked away from them emotionally. Please forgive me."

Dee prayed for many other people and needs that evening. Her thankfulness to the Lord began with her entire family. She concluded that night with, "Lord, time is close for Oklahoma. If it is Your will, please make a way for me to go. I desperately need some encouragement over that 4th of July weekend."

The Lord heard her prayers.

CHAPTER 15

Dee's contact with Tony had decreased once again, since he had moved in with the new girl friend. She continued to hear reports of a pending wedding, although nothing was being said about a divorce.

The Lord seemed to be blocking her trip to Tulsa in every way. Foremost, she had no ticket, nor had she registered. Her car had broken down that preceding week, and since her resident mechanic was out in the far country, she ended up with a big bill from a gas station. The family promising John a place to stay backed out, since they were going out of town themselves.

On the first Friday in July, a dejected Dee, with less than ten dollars in her purse, drove Sylvia to the airport for her flight to Oklahoma. Why had God failed to provide the one thing that Dee both wanted and needed.

"That's it," Dee concluded aloud, while on the trip home. "Tony is history. I give up if the Lord can't even provide a plane ticket, then He probably won't bring my husband home."

That evening, for the first night in months, Dee did not pray for Tony. In fact, she did not pray for anything. Her plans were to call the attorney on Monday, even though she had no money, and somehow divorce Tony. She intended to then start praying for a new man.

A few miles away, Tony Taylor sat in the elegant home of the woman with whom he was living, reading the church page from the newspaper.

Now wait a minute. Are you really that surprised that Tony was reading church news? You have already heard how double minded he was, and that war within him continued to rage. He had no idea why he had even picked up that page, but the Lord did.

Tony saw that his favorite gospel group, a family from east Tennessee was going to be in Hopkinsville on Sunday night for a "Patriotic Concert." The three women and man who sang together had always blessed Dee and Tony. Many times they had driven an hour or more to see them in concert.

Tony was forgetting that he had once told Barney, his friend who died, "If I ever start down the wrong path, just send me to one of their concerts. I always come away blessed and closer to the Lord than when I arrived. That family loves the Lord and they share it."

"Patriotic Concert?" mused Tony. "That sounds harmless. Hopkinsville is far enough away that no one I know will be there. I think I'll go."

Sunday afternoon, Tony made up some kind of believable lie (by now he was quite skilled at that), put on a suit and headed out for Hopkinsville to attend a concert celebrating July 4th.

Driving alone, Tony looked down at his trousers. The suit he had pulled out of Amy's closet was the one that Dee had always called his "gospel suit." He had selected it on his own as a suit for church, but Dee had talked him out of ever wearing it to church. Hot dog mustard could have been dropped all over the front of that suit, and no one would have noticed. The best use for that suit was to wear it to southern gospel concerts, which Tony had done frequently.

Tony dug around between the seats and found a cassette featuring the group that he was going to hear. Here it was July, and he had not listened to one of their tapes since last November, before he moved out. That tape sounded so great that he continued to increase the volume until it was as loud as it would go.

There was prodigal spouse and adulterer Tony Taylor, wearing his "gospel suit." He was on the way to a gospel concert, listening to gospel music as loud as it would go, and singing along with the songs, all of which he knew so well. For just a second, Tony pretended that Dee was sitting beside him, singing her part of the harmony of a song, as she had done so often. Who says that the Lord does not speak to prodigal spouses?

Tony was so engrossed in his thoughts and in his loud music that it took two attempts to get his attention.

"I'll be 10-50 with a speeder," Officer Tremonte reported on the radio as he hit his siren for the second time.

Tony was not as fortunate this time as he had been on the initial meeting with Bud Tremonte. If the officer recognized Tony, he did not say so. After all, Bud had made hundreds of new "friends" along the highway in the past seven months. Tony, however, recognized him immediately.

While the officer was writing a citation, Tony watched him in his cracked rearview mirror. He recalled every word that this man had shared with him seven months ago.

"Could I ever go home to Dee?", Tony asked himself while signing his citation. Tony did not have an opportunity to answer, as the officer was explaining how to satisfy the citation.

As he pulled back onto the highway, he saw Officer Tremonte sitting in his car, completing the paperwork. "No way," he mumbled, "might work for him, but not for me." With that he turned the volume up and punched the gas.

Only then did Bud Tremonte remember their first meeting. He stopped writing on the back of that citation for just a second. *"Lord, help him,"* he prayed, *"bring him to his senses."*

CHAPTER 16

"Dee, Dee, your house is on fire! Are you all right?"

The screams of her neighbor, Mary Humphries, brought Dee back to July 5th. The grill in front of her was ablaze, as was the canopy over it.

The flames were blowing within a couple feet of the porch on her home.

"Dee, get out of there right now! Watch out for the water. We saw the flames and called the fire department." Dee became aware of several sirens off in the distance.

Dee had become so engrossed in thinking about how her family got into that terrible mess, that she had not noticed her hamburgers had caught on fire. The breeze had blown the flames into the awning, catching it on fire. This had all happened within five feet of Dee and she had not even noticed.

Mary and her husband had Dee out of harm's way, and the fire extinguished before the sirens stopped in front of the Taylor's home. Four firemen in bunker gear came running around the house.

Heaped on top of all the other emotions that Dee was experiencing was embarrassment. This all caught up with her, and she suddenly passed out, falling to the grass.

When Dee came to, she was looking into the face of a paramedic, who had been taking her blood pressure. By this time, young John had heard there were fire trucks at his house and had come running home. The parents of the friend Deborah had been visiting had brought her home.

"Lie still. Don't try to get up," the paramedic cautioned.

"Your blood pressure is elevated." Dee looked around and saw that her back yard was full of people. She saw the grill and burned canopy, and suddenly remembered what had happened. Her first thought was to hate Tony more than ever. This was all his fault, and she was not being bashful about declaring that fact to everyone who had gathered because of her crisis. She did not know how the fire was his fault, but she knew that it was. She would figure it out, as soon as things settled down.

Although the paramedics suggested that she go to the hospital, Dee refused to be taken to be checked-out. She wasn't sure if she still had health insurance.

One fireman helped Dee to her feet. Gradually things settled down at the Taylor's. Dee was so proud of John, as he assumed the role of man of the house, and helped straighten the aftereffects of their near disaster.

John was trying to ask his mom what he could fix for their dinner when the phone rang. It was Pastor Wilson calling for her.

"Hi, Dee. Sam and I were wondering if we could come by and see you?"

Dee declined the visit, explaining what had just happened. Pastor Wilson pressed the issue.

"I haven't even fed my kids dinner," she said. "I ruined their great picnic."

"Perfect!" the pastor retorted. "Senior Saints had a picnic today, and left tons of food in the kitchen. I'll run next door to the church and pack up supper for us. You know how much Tony enjoys the food at church dinners."

Reluctantly, she agreed, and started to help John straighten up their home.

"What did he mean, 'You know how much Tony enjoys the food at church dinners?' The guy must have forgotten my husband bailed out on me. This will be a good opportunity for me to tell Sam and the Pastor that I've given up standing."

In a few minutes, Dee heard a car in the driveway and peered out her customary spot in the front drape. She saw Pastor Wilson get out from behind the wheel, and then Sam exit the other side. The back door opened, and getting out of the back seat was TONY!

Her screams brought John and Deborah running to her side, both thinking something had happened to their mom after the fire. Although all three people were walking toward the front door, Dee was frozen.

Tony was wearing his gospel suit. It looked like he had slept in it, but it never looked better. It looked like he had not shaved that day. He was sobbing uncontrollably. Dee noticed that her husband was shaking as he had done at Barney's funeral.

It only takes about half a minute to walk from that driveway to the Taylor's front door, but during that time Dee had about a million different thoughts: "They're coming to tell me something bad. Someone has died!", "He is moving out more things and is using the pastor instead of the police!", "He's taking my kids away!", "He's sold our house!"

Then suddenly she screamed aloud, "What if he is coming home?! I'm not ready. I-I-ah-never thought that--." She did not complete her faithless statement.

John and Deborah went tearing out the front door. Lanky John grabbed his dad so hard that they both almost fell over. Deborah was hugging his legs. It was Deborah who first exclaimed, "Thank you, Jesus, for bringing my daddy home. I knew you would." Dee broke out of her frozen posture at the front door and went running.

As soon as Tony saw her, he fell to his knees, with arms open. Samantha Wilson's tears flowed as her thoughts flashed back to her own dad coming home. Pastor Wilson had set the box containing supper down on the hood of his car and he quietly prayed under his breath.

Tony could only repeat a few words over and over, "I'm sorry. Forgive me. I'm so sorry, forgive me, please forgive me. I'm so sorry."

Dee replied with the correct answer. It was not the "textbook" answer, but The Book answer, coming not from her head, but from her heart. "You were forgiven before I ever saw you getting out of that car. You were forgiven, no matter when the Lord brought you home."

Mary Humphries, from next door, heard all the commotion and looked out her window. "You won't believe it," she called out to husband number two. "The guy is down on his knees begging Dee to take him back. I sure hope she doesn't, because no matter what she does, it won't work. I know from experience."

Yes, Mary, you are correct. No matter what she does, it won't work. But once Jesus comes by, and Tony and Dee turn to Him, it won't fail.

Several months later, when Mary's number two husband jumped ship, it was to Dee to whom she turned. There is someone else living in that house next door now. Dee had led Mary to the Lord, and back to her covenant husband.

Dee's rejoicing party made its way into the Taylor home a few steps at a time. Tony was too broken-up to relate what had happened. Dee sat in her chair, with Tony on the floor next to her, his arm across her lap.

Out of joy, young Deborah was doing what she had seen her mother do so many times as she passed out tissue. She stopped at her father to give him a hug. Her, "I love you Daddy," reopened his floodgate of tears.

"Tony, may I tell Dee what has happened?", Pastor Wilson asked. The only response Tony could give was an affirming nod.

"Last evening," he began, "Tony went to Hopkinsville for a gospel concert. He thought that he was going to a patriotic concert, but the Holy Spirit of God met him there. Tony told me that every song the family sang was used by God to touch his heart more than the previous."

"When your husband heard a song about feet weary from the mountain that's been climbed, he began to talk to the Lord for the first time in a long while. Tony was asking the Lord if he could ever change. Then he became aware they were singing about Jesus coming down the road, right on time. Dee, your husband met Jesus last night, right on time."

"I hope some day those hillbillies know how they touched me," Tony sobbed.

"Your husband knew that he could not go back to where he had been living, so he slept in his car last night," Pastor Wilson continued. "This morning, he drove by the church, desperate for help. Sam and I were out in our yard when he saw us and stopped."

"When I got out of the car and she said, 'Hi, Tony.' I never met her before, but--," with that he went back to his sobs of repentance.

"I spent all morning working and praying with Tony. We did serious business about the issues in his life."

"You mean about the dirty pictures?", an innocent Deborah mumbled, while eating a sandwich that Samantha had put together for her.

"Yes Honey," a shocked pastor responded, "about the dirty pictures. Jesus brought your Daddy home, but he also took away those pictures forever. He has forgiven your Daddy."

"Dee, I knew that Tony was serious about doing business with the Lord, but I asked him to put actions behind his words. I called the senior pastor and obtained permission for Tony to use the missionary's efficiency at church for a few weeks."

"I told Tony that if he was serious, I would support him one hundred percent if he would make himself accountable to me for a period. I asked him to go move out of the other woman's house and live right at the church, as my next door neighbor. Tony was back in an hour, and Sam and I helped him get settled in."

Right at that moment, the Holy Spirit had given Pastor Wilson an illustration. "Tony," he asked, "have you ever done any body work on those cars at the shop?"

"A little, but I have friends who do," Tony replied with a great snort. He seemed to welcome the change in topic from his homecoming.

"How is their work?"

"Sometimes better than the original!"

"So when a car is brought in with rust damage from the salt put on roads in winter, they slap some of that gray stuff over the damage, and then finish it off, right?"

"No way, the rust would eat through again. The body guys go in, digging out and cutting away all the rust. They then use the 'gray stuff,' as you call it, to fill the hole, sand it off and finish it."

"Tony, I couldn't have said it better myself. You have presented your rusted soul to our Holy God who will be digging out and cutting away everything impure. Then He will smooth out all the rough areas and give you a new finish. I can promise, by the authority of Holy Scripture, that you will look better than you have ever looked before."

The pastor's illustration had been interrupted by the telephone ringing.

"Dee, this is Sylvia. Did you forget to pick me up?"

"I'll be at the airport in fifteen minutes. Something has happened." Dee explained to the Wilsons and to her husband, who Sylvia was and where she had been. The pastor offered to drive her to the airport, and both couples loaded into the pastor's car.

Sylvia was waiting on the curb, her suitcase next to her.

"Hi Dee! I hate to tell you what you missed. It was a blessed time. Next year I will see to it that you get to Oklahoma. Do I ever have a lot to tell you about...the ministry, the singing, and all the standers I met!"

Sylvia noticed three other people getting out of this strange car. "Sylvia, I would like to introduce you to my pastor and his wife." Sylvia thought how nice it was that Dee's pastor had driven her to the airport, but she could not understand why they had brought a bum with them. This character had on the ugliest suit that she had ever seen! It was mustard colored and had not seen an iron in weeks. There were grass stains all over the knees. His hair was rumpled and he needed a shave. And the guy had a goofy-looking grin on his face! Sylvia could only imagine how that car must smell with him inside.

"Sylvia, I would like for you to meet my husband, Tony."

Her friend was speechless. Finally, she gave Tony a big hug. He smelled so sweet.

Dee offered the short version of the past 24 hours, "Satan even tried to burn my house down when my husband was on the way home, but he is defeated by the blood of Jesus." They all climbed in the car and started home. It seemed that everyone was talking at once almost all the way.

Pastor Wilson did indeed work with Tony, allowing God to cut, and dig and sand. One step at a time, Tony was restored to his place of spiritual leadership in his family, and later, in his church.

On the day that Tony "officially" moved home, Pastor Wilson officiated at the renewal of their wedding vows before a full church. Several men shared with Tony what an encouragement he had been.

"Uh Rev, my name is Mitch," one man introduced himself to Pastor Wilson. "I work with Tony. Me and my girlfriend want to get baptized. We came to church here last week and we prayed to receive Jesus. You can ask Tony about us, and tell him I cleaned off the coffee table."

The eternal results of all that Tony and Dee had gone through were only beginning. To God be the glory!

A year later, the couple to whom the Lord had entrusted with His marriage ministry down in Florida, were updating their mailing list. Standers would move and forget to let them know. Others would have their marriage healed and forget to let them know.

"Dee Taylor from Paducah," the husband offered, "she used to write all the time, but we haven't heard from her in a year.

To be good stewards of God's money, I guess we need to remove her from the newsletter list."

"Let's just pray that she hasn't been deceived by the enemy to give up her stand," his wife replied.

No, Dee has not given up her stand. Her prodigal came home and she forgot to let you know. Dee and Tony are doing fine. Like all couples being restored, they have ups and downs, but they always turn to Jesus and He always helps.

Tony's bondage of addiction to pornography has been broken. He has also helped a few other men with that problem as well. The guys at work still call Tony, "Preacher Man," but now it is out of respect, not out of jest.

"Yes, I'm still standing," Dee later wrote in a letter being sent to Florida. "Tony came home on July 4th weekend last year, and I continue to stand and fight that spiritual battle for my family until Jesus comes, or He calls one of us home."

Three days later, down in Pompano Beach, a RESTORED' sticker was pasted on the Taylor's family photo hanging on the wall of a ministry office.

By the way, they have another of those RESTORED! stickers set aside just for you, SO DON'T GIVE UP!

THERE IS FREEDOM IN CHRIST

A Word From Charlyne

It is for freedom that Christ has set us free... **Galatians 5:1**

As you have been reading this book, has the Lord been dealing with your heart? I thank the Lord that He has allowed you to read this book to give you hope and encouragement for you and your marriage. You are thinking, "But, you don't know my circumstances, they are *even worse* than Tony's." That may be true, but I know the God I serve. I know the power of my awesome, mighty God.

"...Then you will know that I am the Lord; those who hope in me will not be disappointed." **Isaiah 49:23**

You, your spouse or your loved ones *can* be set free from bondages, addictions, strongholds and sins that have come into their lives. **They can be set free** from the enemy through the **power of your Lord Jesus Christ.**

"...With man this is impossible, but not with God; all things are possible with God." **Mark 10:27**

When the Lord touched me after I had divorced Bob, I was a Christian, but I did not have a personal relationship with my Lord. I knew Jesus as my Savior, but did not believe that Jesus could solve any of my daily routine problems. I did not know Him as the Lord of my life. Where are you spiritually? How do you know Jesus? Have you turned your life over to Jesus as Savior of your life? Do you know Him as Lord of your life? Do you read His love letters to you and talk to Him daily?

"...I tell you the truth, no one can see the kingdom of God unless he is born again." **John 3:3**

"For God so loved the world that he gave his one and only Son, that whoever believes in him shall not perish but have eternal life." **John 3:16**

You may have accepted the Lord when you were a child and backslidden or you may have never prayed a prayer of repentance. Regardless of whom your parents or grandparents are, you must confess your sins and repent, asking your Lord Jesus Christ to come into your heart. As an adult, do you know for certain that if you should die today, that you would go to heaven? If not, right now, before you finish reading this book, stop and confess your sins, repent and turn from any ways that are not pleasing to your Heavenly Father.

..."Everyone who calls on the name of the Lord will be saved." **Romans 10:13**

God wants to give you the answers to the questions and problems of your life. He wants to give you the power to overcome difficulties and circumstances.

If we confess our sins, he is faithful and just and will forgive us our sins and purify us from all unrighteousness.
1 John 1:9

Now that you are born again you have a second decision. Surrender your life completely to Him and walk in His footsteps every day. Let Him be the Lord of your life. He is giving you the Holy Spirit to be with you forever. He will be your Lord, your Heavenly Father, your spouse for a season, your Counselor, your Shepherd, your Protector, your Provider, your Healer and everything you need in your life.

"If you love me, you will obey what I command. And I will ask the Father, and he will give you another Counselor to be with you forever--the Spirit of truth. ...But the Counselor, the Holy Spirit, whom the Father will send in my name, will teach you all things and will remind you of everything I have said to

you." **John 14:15-17, 26**

"But you will receive power when the Holy Spirit comes on you; and you will be my witnesses in Jerusalem, and in all Judea and Samaria, and to the ends of the earth." **Acts 1:8**

Bob and I are deeply burdened about the epidemic of divorce in the United States and in the world. Divorce used to happen to the unchurched, but now divorce in the church is just as common as in the world.

My people are destroyed from lack of knowledge.... **Hosea 4:6**

The god of this age has blinded the minds of unbelievers, so that they cannot see the light of the gospel of the glory of Christ, who is the image of God. **2 Corinthians 4:4**

What can you or I do? We need to take a stand for marriages throughout the nation. Are you willing to join God's army to fight the fight against the enemy? I believe that your Lord is knocking at your heart's door asking you to join with other standers to stand in the gap for ALL prodigals that are away from their families. We need to learn how to pray, and fight the enemy. Satan is defeated, Christians need to know and walk in TRUTH!

Ask the Lord to use you as a lighthouse in your home, in your family, in your church, in your city and in your state, proclaiming that God hates divorce. There is another way: God's way!

"Yet if there is an angel on his side as a mediator, one out of a thousand, to tell a man what is right for him, to be gracious to him and say, 'Spare him from going down to the pit; I have found a ransom for him'--then his flesh is renewed like a child's; it is restored as in the days of his youth. He prays to God and finds favor with him, he sees God's face and shouts for

joy; he is restored by God to his righteous state. Then he comes to men and says, 'I sinned, and perverted what was right, but I did not get what I deserved. He redeemed my soul from going down to the pit, and I will live to enjoy the light.'"
Job 33:23-28

This scripture is truly the testimony of every prodigal who has repented and has come home to the Lord and to his family!

Are you ready to join the Lord's army?

JOIN GOD'S ARMY!

... 'Do not be afraid or discouraged because of the vast army. For the battle is not yours, but God's.'
2 Chronicles 20:15

Is your marriage hopeless and dead by the world's standards? If so, you can join God's army and have Him restore and put new life into your dead marriage.

Allow the Holy Spirit to show you His power in defeating the enemy. **Read 2 Chronicles 20**. Allow the Holy Spirit to show you His plan and strategy. Here is a brief outline to help:

- Face the problem or circumstance.

- Seek the Lord, praying and fasting for His direction.

- God is Faithful.

- Know His power over all people and circumstances.

- Cry out to Him and He will hear you.

- Believe and stand on the promises of God.

- Worship your Lord having faith in His power.

- Praise the Lord in faith and in obedience.

- God's presence means deliverance and victory.

Do you know how to pray for your spouse or prodigal? Are you tired of praying? Do you know anything about spiritual warfare? This chapter is going to be your beginner's manual for boot camp in the Lord's army. Ask God to give you wisdom and knowledge to be able to fight for your loved ones.

FACE THE PROBLEM

Jehoshaphat faced a great crisis. Is that how you feel right now? Your spouse may be involved in adultery or may be addicted to pornography, gambling, sexual sins, alcohol, drugs or a combination of these sins. Do not be afraid or discouraged. Your Lord God is with you, right now, and He will never leave you or forsake you.

I will say of the Lord, "He is my refuge and my fortress, my God, in whom I trust." Surely he will save you from the fowler's snare and from the deadly pestilence. He will cover you with his feathers, and under his wings you will find refuge; his faithfulness will be your shield and rampart."
Psalm 91:2-4

God has a plan and a purpose for you and your family even though you are in the midst of severe marriage problems.

*"For I know the plans I have for you," declares the Lord, "plans to prosper you and not to harm you, plans to give you hope and a future. Then you will call upon me and come and pray to me, and I will listen to you. You will seek me and find me when you seek me with all your heart." **Jeremiah 29:11-13***

Jehoshaphat was alarmed. You may be alarmed, afraid or in shock and hurting. You need to humble yourself and ask the Lord, what He wants you to do.

SEEK THE LORD BY PRAYING AND FASTING

Jehoshaphat called his people together to proclaim a fast and seek help from the Lord. May you seek the Lord for His help, fasting and praying. You may have never fasted for yourself or your loved ones. I had not. The Lord directed me to 2 Chronicles 20 early in my journey with Him. He used that scripture to give me guidelines to learn how to fight for my spouse and my family. Ask the Lord what He would have you to do.

"Is not this the kind of fasting I have chosen; to loose the chains of injustice and untie the cords of the yoke, to set the oppressed free and break every yoke?" **Isaiah 58:6**

GOD IS FAITHFUL

'If calamity comes upon us, whether the sword of judgment, or plague or famine, we will stand in your presence before this temple that bears your Name and will cry out to you in our distress, and you will hear us and save us.'
2 Chronicles 20:9

For the word of the Lord is right and true; he is faithful in all he does. **Psalm 33:4**

KNOW THE POWER OF GOD

"... O Lord, God of our fathers, are you not the God who is in heaven? You rule over all the kingdoms of the nations. Power and might are in your hand, and no one can withstand you." **2 Chronicles 20:6**

God is our refuge and strength, an ever present help in trouble. ... "Be still, and know that I am God; I will be exalted among the nations, I will be exalted in the earth." **The Lord**

Almighty is with us; the God of Jacob is our fortress.   Selah
Psalm 46:1,10-11

I want to stand in agreement with you for a miracle from God, because I know My Lord and My God. He is an awesome mighty God. He created the heavens and the earth. He can make crooked paths straight. He sent His son to die on the cross for ALL sinners. I know He loves you and your spouse. He will never leave you or forsake you.

I can say that my divorce was the best thing that happened to me as I was able to meet my Lord God in a way that I had never known Him. Today, my relationship with the Lord is more important than my spouse, children, or career. He must be first in your life. Then He will give you the desires of your heart. **He is the only one who has the power to change your spouse's heart!**

Wash away all my iniquity and cleanse me from my sin...
Create in me a pure heart, O God, and renew a steadfast spirit
within me...Restore to me the joy of your salvation and grant me
a willing spirit, to sustain me. **Psalm 51:2, 10, 12**

CRY OUT TO HIM

God is waiting for you to come to Him. He created you to have a personal relationship with Him. The Lord is waiting for you to come to Him seeking to know Him better. Do you know the voice of God? Can you hear Him? Spend time telling the Lord your every hurt and need. Talking to Him will give you a peace that is beyond understanding. Ask God to direct your every step.

"... For we have no power to face this vast army that is
attacking us. We do not know what to do, but our eyes are upon
you." **2 Chronicles 20:12**

BELIEVE AND STAND
ON THE PROMISES OF GOD.

I cannot emphasize too strongly the importance of God's Word and the power of that Word. I do not think I will ever comprehend the extent of the power of God until I meet my Lord in Heaven. The Lord started speaking to me through reading His Word. Scriptures would seem to leap off the page to touch me. I would write down questions in my journal, or cry out my hurts and needs, then start reading the Word and scriptures would answer my questions. My Lord was talking to me! When this happened, I knew that I knew that it was God.

I pray that you will experience this as well. Once you try it, you will never again want to take surveys of friends, family, counselors, and pastors to see how to deal with a prodigal spouse. The Lord God has the answer to everything.

"My sheep listen to my voice; I know them, and they follow me." **John 10:27**

"...This is what the Lord says to you: 'Do not be afraid or discouraged because of this vast army. For the battle is not yours but God's....You will not have to fight this battle. Take up your positions; stand firm and see the deliverance the Lord will give you, O Judah and Jerusalem. Do not be afraid; do not be discouraged. Go out to face them tomorrow, and the Lord will be with you.'" **2 Chronicles 20:15,17**

WORSHIP YOUR LORD;
HAVE FAITH IN HIS POWER

Bob was gone for two years. Over and over again, my Lord showed me His power. I can say today that I have more faith in my Lord than in anything else or in anyone else. He can do anything!

Ten years after our remarriage, when Bob suffered a stroke and was fighting for his life, I turned to my Lord to seek His face and ask Him for His will to be done in that circumstance. **He has the power over everything because He created everything!**

Jehoshaphat bowed with his face to the ground, and all the people of Judah and Jerusalem fell down in worship before the Lord.... "Have faith in the Lord your God and you will be upheld; have faith in his prophets and you will successful." **2 Chronicles 20:18,20**

PRAISE THE LORD
IN FAITH AND IN OBEDIENCE

When you start seeking the Lord, He starts talking to you showing you His will and way for your life. You have a choice. Do you have faith in your Lord to be obedient to His commands? Just as your prodigal is in the far country, you can also be disobedient by not listening and obeying the Lord. Noah had a choice whether to build an ark as the Lord requested Him to do or listen to his human understanding and other peoples' opinions. No one knew what the Lord was going to do. No one knew about rain or the floods. Noah had to have faith in His Lord and be obedient. Are you willing to do the same?

...Jehoshaphat appointed men to sing to the Lord and to praise him for the splendor of his holiness as they went out at the head of the army, saying: "Give thanks to the Lord, for his love endures forever." **2 Chronicles 20:21**

GOD'S PRESENCE MEANS
DELIVERANCE AND VICTORY

The Lord loves your spouse more than you do. Jesus

defeated satan when he was tempted by using the Word of the Lord. Jesus died on the cross for everyone, defeating satan, showing God's power even after death! Nothing is too hard for your God. He uses different people and circumstances to bring deliverance and victory for each of His children.

As they began to sing and praise, the Lord set ambushes against the men of Ammon and Moab and Mount Seir who were invading Judah, and they were defeated. **2 Chronicles 20:22**

Commit to the Lord whatever you do, and your plans will succeed. **Proverbs 16:3**

When a man's ways are pleasing to the Lord, he makes even his enemies live at peace with him. **Proverbs 16:7**

Are you ready to join God's army? Will you become a mighty soldier, a warrior and an intercessor for God's army?

WHO IS THE ENEMY?

I was devastated when we were having marriage problems. I thought that I had given one hundred and ten percent to our marriage. I had tried to do everything that would please Bob. Regardless of all my efforts, Bob was miserable. He was unhappy, he was angry, he was depressed, and he was critical of everything I did. Due to Bob's sinful nature, he was abusive in his behavior. I did not know what to do. I loved him one minute, then hated his behavior the next.

Before we divorced in 1985, we sought out many Christian counselors and pastors, seeking help. They each were very sorry for our circumstances, but did not share any scriptures or tell us how to accomplish the changes that were needed.

None of our counselors gave us guidance on how to get Bob to become the spiritual head of our home or how to remove the strife in our home. They did say to me, "You are responsible for your children. You do not want your children exposed to his sin."

We were the perfect-looking "Ozzie and Harriet" family at church, but behind closed doors at home, we were in a battle throughout the week. Sadly, this is the plight of many Christian families today, but our Lord Jesus has the solution.

Why were we that way? We loved each other, but throughout our marriage there was always something that was not right. What was it? Why couldn't we have a good marriage? The Lord revealed the answers after Bob was gone.

The first few months after our final separation, I felt a failure. I was angry and bitter at Bob for allowing his selfishness to cause him to give up on our marriage. He was going on with his life, dating and changing his lifestyle. I was left at home with three children, the bills, and the daily responsibility of raising and providing for our children. What happened to our marriage after we walked down the aisle in my wedding gown and his tux?

We have an altar in the front of our church. Every week at prayer time, I went and wept loudly, crying out for the Lord to help me through this crisis of our marriage problems, during our separation. I could not hear anything. I proceeded to divorce Bob due to his unfaithfulness, which the pastor, counselor and all our church friends said was alright. I was the "innocent victim."

What happened to our marriage after our wedding day? What has happened to fifty percent of all the marriages throughout the country after their wedding day? Did we all marry the wrong person? NO!!! **Our homes are being attacked by the enemy**.

The enemy tempted my husband and many other spouses throughout the world to things of the world. Bob, nor other spouses, think it will hurt anyone. They did not know the consequences. Have you opened your home to the enemy? Who is the enemy?

Be self-controlled and alert. Your enemy the devil prowls around like a roaring lion looking for someone to devour. Resist him, standing firm in the faith, because you know that your brothers throughout the world are undergoing the same kind of sufferings. I Peter 5:8-9

Peter warns us to watch out for satan, especially if we are suffering. If we are feeling alone, weak, or helpless,

We see the enemy, the serpent, in the very first book of the Bible. He tempted Eve, and she was deceived and fell into sin, which was the fall of man.

Then the Lord God said to the woman, "What is this you

*have done?" The woman said, "The serpent deceived me, and I ate." **Genesis 3:13***

What lies and what mistakes have you made when you listened to the enemy?

SATAN IS THE ENEMY

The devil, or satan, has many different names: the enemy, the avenger, adversary, the accuser, the tempter, prince of this world, god of this age, father of all lies, murderer, the ruler of the kingdom of the air, dragon, ancient serpent, Lucifer, star of the morning, and angel of light.

*How you are fallen from heaven, O morning star, son of the dawn! You have been cast down to the earth, you who once laid low the nations! You said in your heart, "I will ascend to heaven; I will raise my throne above the stars of God; I will sit enthroned on the mount of assembly, on the utmost heights of the sacred mountain. I will ascend above the tops of the clouds; I will make myself like the Most High." But you are brought down to the grave, to the depths of the pit. **Isaiah 14:12-15***

*And there was war in heaven. Michael and his angels fought against the dragon, and the dragon and his angels fought back. But he was not strong enough, and they lost their place in heaven. The great dragon was hurled down--that ancient serpent called the devil, or Satan, who leads the whole world astray. He was hurled to the earth, and his angels with him. **Revelation 12:7-9***

*"You belong to your father, the devil, and you want to carry out your father's desire. He was a murderer from the beginning, not holding to the truth, for there is no truth in him. When he lies, he speaks his native language, for he is a liar and the father of lies." **John 8:44***

He (Jesus) replied, "I saw Satan fall like lightening from heaven. I have given you authority to trample on snakes and scorpions, and to overcome all the power of the enemy; nothing will harm you. However, do not rejoice that the spirits submit to you, but rejoice that your names are written in heaven."
Luke 10:18-20

JESUS WAS ALSO TEMPTED BY THE DEVIL

Then Jesus was led by the Spirit into the desert to be tempted by the devil. After fasting forty days and forty nights, he was hungry. The tempter came to him and said, "If you are the Son of God, tell these stones to become bread." Jesus answered, "It is written; 'Man does not live on bread alone, but on every word that comes from the mouth of God.' " ...Jesus said to him, "Away from me, Satan! For it is written: 'Worship the Lord your God, and serve him only.' " Then the devil left him, and angels came and attended him. **Matthew 4:1-4,10-11**

We each need to know that we do not have to listen to satan's temptations. We need to be aware of the enemy as to his purpose to destroy all of us.

"The thief comes only to steal and kill and destroy. I have come that they may have life, and have it to the full."
John 10:10

OUR LORD GOD IS FAITHFUL.

So, if you think you are standing firm, be careful that you don't fall! No temptation has seized you except what is common to man. And God is faithful; he will not let you be tempted beyond what you can bear. But when you are tempted, he will also provide a way out so that you can stand up under it. **1 Corinthians 10:12-13**

*...The Lord is faithful to all his promises and loving toward all he has made. **Psalm 145:13***

JESUS PRAYED FOR HIS DISCIPLES

*"All I have is yours, and all you have is mine. And glory has come to me through them. I will remain in the world no longer, but they are still in the world, and I am coming to you. Holy Father, protect them by the power of your name--the name you gave me--so that they may be one as we are one. While I was with them, I protected them and kept them safe by that name you gave me...." **John 17:10-12***

HE HEARS OUR CRIES

*"... Never will I leave you; never will I forsake you." So we say with confidence, "The Lord is my helper; I will not be afraid. What can man do to me?" **Hebrews 13:5-6***

OUR LORD IS GREATER THAN THE ENEMY

We do not have to REACT TO THE ATTACKS OF THE ENEMY. ALLOW THE LORD TO RESCUE YOU FROM THE ENEMY. We need to be obedient to the Lord! Ask for the Lord's daily direction and guidance in your life.

*Rescue me from my enemies, O Lord, for I hide myself in you. Teach me to do your will, for you are my God; may your good Spirit lead me on level ground. **Psalm 143:9-10***

If you make the Most High your dwelling--even the Lord, who is my refuge--then no harm will befall you, no disaster will come near your tent. For he will command his angels concerning you to guard you in all your ways; they will lift you up in their hands, so that you will not strike your foot against a stone. You will tread upon the lion and the cobra; you will trample the great lion and the serpent. "Because he loves me," says the Lord, "I will rescue him; I will protect him, for he acknowledges my name. He will call upon me, and I will answer him; I will be with him in trouble, I will deliver him and honor him." **Psalm 91:9-15**

After our divorce, I thought the enemy was my husband, but then the Lord revealed the truth. He gave me scriptures to show me that my spouse was not my enemy. The Lord also showed me that we were conquerors in Jesus Christ. He left us weapons to fight the enemy.

For our struggle is not against flesh and blood, but against the rulers, against the authorities, against the powers of this dark world and against the spiritual forces of evil in the heavenly realms. **Ephesians 6:12**

... If God is for us, who can be against us?... No, in all these things we are more than conquerors through him who loved us. For I am convinced that neither death or life, neither angels nor demons, neither the present nor the future, nor any powers, neither height nor depth, nor anything else in all creation, will be able to separate us from the love of God that is in Christ Jesus our Lord. **Romans 8:31,37-39**

Now that you know who the enemy is, let us learn to become a prayer warrior in God's army. We cannot just be passive, we need to be aggressive. We need to stand firm. Do not let the enemy take anymore territory from your family. We need to be like the disciples after Pentecost and be **bold** in the Lord.

Tell the enemy he is not touching anything or anyone else in your family! We need to stand in the gap pleading our spouse's and loved ones' cases before our Heavenly Father. Stand on the Word of God and the enemy will be defeated in God's timing!

YOU ARE IN A SPIRITUAL BATTLE

After Bob and I were divorced I thought I would feel better, the pain in my heart would go away. There was no fighting in our home, but something was wrong. My husband and the father of my children was missing. Deep inside I still loved him very much. What happened to our marriage vows, *"For better or worse, richer or poor, in sickness or in health, til death us do part?"* I kept crying out to my Lord asking, "Why, what happened?" Many people would tell me that Bob had his own free will and I could do nothing to change his mind. They told me "Get on with your life." The pain in my heart would never leave. I asked the Lord, "What should I do?"

Then the Lord showed me His answer. He sent a couple, Paul and Ann Downing, to share their testimony at our church. He had been an alcoholic, abusive and unfaithful for quite a period of time. Ann did not give up on Paul, as I had given up on Bob and on God. Ann shared that she fasted and would lie prostrate on the floor, pleading for Paul's salvation and deliverance from the enemy. Then the Lord touched him, saved and delivered him.

The Downings then went around the country singing and sharing their testimony of the power of their God. The Lord called Paul home a few years ago. Before he died, he saw Bob's first book, *Prodigals Do Come Home*, and heard how the the Lord used their testimony to reach us.

After I heard their testimony, I knew that I had failed God and Bob. I did not fast and pray for my spouse. I gave up on God and on Bob due to the circumstances and the opinions of so many people. I realized that I was the one going home alone with all the responsibilities that God had created two people to carry together. Marriage was created by God. Divorce is caused by the enemy and people's sinfulness.

Has not the Lord made them one? In flesh and spirit they

are his. And why one? Because he was seeking godly offspring. So guard yourself in your spirit, and do not break faith with the wife of your youth. "I hate divorce," says the Lord God of Israel.... **Malachi 2:15-16**

That Sunday evening, I went to the altar, repenting of my lack of knowledge and for my part in the failure of our marriage. I forgave Bob for all that he had done and was doing to our family. I realized that Bob did not know that the enemy had come against our home. The Lord gave me a scripture to confirm all that He had shown me.

Flee the evil desires of youth, and pursue righteousness, faith, love and peace, along with those who call on the Lord out of a pure heart. Don't have anything to do with foolish and stupid arguments, because you know they produce quarrels. And the Lord's servant must not quarrel; instead, he must be kind to everyone, able to teach, not resentful. Those who oppose him he must gently instruct, in the hope that God will grant them repentance leading them to a knowledge of the truth, and that they will come to their senses and escape from the trap of the devil, who has taken them captive to do his will.
2 Timothy 2:22-26

STAND IN THE GAP

The Lord showed me that He wanted me *to stand in the gap* for our marriage. He loved my husband even more than I did. The Lord asked me if I was willing to pay the price of sacrifice, praying for my spouse's soul.

"I looked for a man among them who would build up the wall and stand before me in the gap on behalf of the land so I would not have to destroy it, but I found none." **Ezekiel 22:30**

If a burglar had come into our home with a gun and taken Bob hostage, would I not pray and fast for his return? The devil came in blinding, deceiving, and tempting my husband to sins of the world due to doorways that he had opened up in his life as a teenager. He also was suffering from the generational sins that had been passed down even from his grandfather.

*"...Yet he does not leave the guilty unpunished; he punishes the children and their children for the sin of the fathers to the third and fourth generation." **Exodus 34:7***

The Lord gave me a hunger and thirst for His Word. He gave me a burden, not only for my husband but also for other marriages that were being destroyed by the enemy.

Other church couples could list many reasons that they divorced, but the real reason was that the enemy found someone who would allow satan to tempt them to fall into the trap of sin. **The good news is that our Lord God is raising up a standard of prayer warriors today to fight for all prodigal spouses and marriages throughout the land.**

Yes, this is a real battle. We need to know both the enemy as well as the weapons of warfare that the Lord has given us to fight the enemy.

During His ministry on earth, our Lord Jesus touched, healed and delivered people from demons. We also know the Lord has left us with the Holy Spirit to do the same today. The question we must each ask ourselves is, "Do I really believe in the power of our Lord God? Do I have enough faith?" What is your answer?

*"...I tell you the truth, If you have faith as small as a mustard seed, you can say to this mountain, 'Move from here to there' and it will move. Nothing will be impossible for you." **Matthew 17:20-21***

The enemy is always trying to deceive God's children. Jesus Christ paid the price and defeated satan at Calvary through the blood of Jesus. We now must maintain the victory that was won.

The Lord has given us spiritual weapons to use to fight the fight. Do you use them? We are to fight the fight in the spiritual realm not in the natural realm.   Are you ready to fight in God's army?

WEAPONS OF OUR WARFARE

THE POWER OF PRAYER

The first and most powerful weapon we need to use is **PRAYER**. The enemy often keeps Christians so busy, we do not take time to pray. This is a trick from the enemy. We need to know that it is vital for each of us to make time to pray. **There is power in prayer**. Only God knows what we do not have, because we do not pray.

"If my people, who are called by my name, will humble themselves and pray and seek my face and turn from their wicked ways, then will I hear from heaven and will forgive their sin and will heal their land. Now my eyes will be open and my ears attentive to the prayers offered in this place."
2 Chronicles 7:14-15

...The prayer of a righteous man is powerful and effective.... My brothers, if one of you should wander from the truth and someone should bring him back, remember this; Whoever turns a sinner from the error of his way will save him from death and cover over a multitude of sins.
James 5:16, 19-20

OUR WEAPONS HAVE DIVINE POWER

As you stand in the gap for your loved ones, the Lord will continue to mature you in the Lord. You have been chosen by God to serve in His army. He will continue to deepen your walk with Him. He will also continue to give you wisdom and knowledge from on High to know how to pray for your family. He has given us the Holy Spirit to empower each of us.

"But you will receive power when the Holy Spirit comes on you; and you will be my witnesses in Jerusalem, and in all

*Judea and Samaria, and to the ends of the earth." **Acts 1:8***

ARMOR OF GOD

If we are going to fight the spiritual battle that has come against our family as well as many other families throughout the world, we need to be dressed properly. A good soldier always has his weapons ready. We need to put on our armor of God daily. Your armor will protect you against the strategies and schemes of the devil. Wear your armor and be ready for battle.

For though we live in the world, we do not wage war as the world does. The weapons we fight with are not the weapons of the world. On the contrary, they have divine power to demolish strongholds. We demolish arguments and every pretension that sets itself up against the knowledge of God, and we take captive every thought to make it obedient to Christ.
2 Corinthians 10:3-5

No weapon formed against you will prosper. ***Isaiah 54:17***

PUT ON YOUR SPIRITUAL ARMOR

*Finally, be strong in the Lord and in his mighty power. Put on the full armor of God so that you can take your stand against the devil's schemes. For our struggle is not against flesh and blood, but against the rulers, against the authorities, against the powers of this dark world and against the spiritual forces of evil in the heavenly realms. Therefore put on the full armor of God, so that when the day of evil comes, you may be able to stand your ground, and after you have done everything, to stand. Stand firm then, with the **belt of truth** buckled around your waist, with the **breastplate of righteousness** in place, and with your **feet fitted with the readiness that comes from the gospel of peace**. In addition to all this, take up **the shield of faith,** with which you can extinguish all the flaming arrows of* *the evil one. Take **the helmet of salvation** and **the sword of the Spirit,** which is the word of God. And pray in the Spirit on all occasions with all kinds of prayers and requests...* **Ephesians 6:10-18**

For the word of God is living and active. Sharper than any double-edged sword, it penetrates even to dividing soul and spirit, joints and marrow; it judges the thoughts and attitudes of the heart. **Hebrews 4:12**

FAITH AND OBEDIENCE

Now faith is being sure of what we hope for and certain of what we do not see. **Hebrews 11:1**

You need to have faith and be obedient. Do you have faith? The opposite of faith is fear, doubt and unbelief.

"Have faith in God," Jesus answered. "I tell you the truth, if anyone says to this mountain, 'Go, throw yourself into the sea,' and does not doubt in his heart but believes that what he says will happen, it will be done for him. Therefore I tell you, whatever you ask for in prayer, believe that you have received it, and it will be yours. And when you stand praying, if you hold anything against anyone, forgive him, so that your Father in heaven may forgive you your sins." **Mark 11:22-25**

We must forgive anyone who has sinned against us, so that our sins may be forgiven by our Heavenly Father. If we do not forgive, we will start to harbor bitterness, resentment and animosity, which are not Christlike. Is there someone you need to go forgive? We need to be obedient and forgive the other person, and allow the Lord touch and change our heart.

THE NAME OF JESUS

There is power in the Name of Jesus. There is no other name like Jesus. When you feel depressed or overwhelmed by your circumstances, just call on Jesus. The powerful name of Jesus will defeat the enemy. You often hear when people are sick, if they will just call on the name of Jesus repeatedly, they will receive a peace that is beyond understanding.

Then Peter said, "Silver or gold I do not have, but what I have I give you. In the name of Jesus Christ of Nazareth, walk." **Acts 3:6**

They had Peter and John brought before them and began to question them: "By what power or what name did you do this?". ... "If we are being called to account today for an act of kindness shown to a cripple and are asked how he was healed, then know this, you and Israel: It is by the name of Jesus Christ of Nazareth, whom you crucified but whom God raised from the dead, that this man stands before you completely healed. **Acts 4:7,9-10**

"I have given you authority to trample on snakes and scorpions and to overcome all the power of the enemy; nothing will harm you." **Luke 10:19**

"And I will do whatever you ask in my name, so that the Son may bring glory to the Father. You may ask me for anything in my name, and I will do it." **John 14:13-14**

Therefore God exalted him to the highest place and gave him the name that is above every name, that at the name of Jesus every knee should bow, in heaven and on earth and under the earth. **Philippians 2:9-10**

THE BLOOD OF JESUS

There is power in the Blood of Jesus. If we obey the Lord, He will give us protection through the blood. The Israelites were protected by the blood of the Lamb. God passed over all the houses that had blood on the sides and tops of the doorframes which protected their firstborns. If the Israelites had not obeyed God and stayed in their houses that night, they would have suffered because of their disobedience.

"They overcame him by the blood of the Lamb and by the word of their testimony...." **Revelation 12:11**

HEDGE OF PROTECTION

If your spouse has been unfaithful, do not look at the circumstances. Believe in the power of your God. The Lord had me say the following scripture in a prayer regularly which I personalized. What a promise! Gomer was told to love Hosea unconditionally. Ask your Heavenly Father to give you the unconditional love that you need for your spouse.

"Therefore I will block her path with thornbushes; I will wall her in so that she cannot find her way. She will chase after her lovers but not catch them; she will look for them but not find them. Then she will say, 'I will go back to my husband as at first, for then I was better off than now.' " **Hosea 2:6-7**

BINDING AND LOOSING

"I tell you the truth, whatever you bind on earth will be bound in heaven, and whatever you loose on earth will be loosed in heaven." **Matthew 18:18**

When we are binding, we are binding the enemy or the strongman. When you are loosing, you are loosing the Holy

Spirit in you and/or your spouse's life.

A book that helped me during my stand in understanding which spirits to bind as in pornography is titled *Strongman's His Name...What's His Game?* It was written by Doctors Jerry and Carol Robeson.

A scripture I have often prayed for myself, my husband and children is **Galatians 5:19-23.** I would bind the sinful nature and loose the fruits of the Holy Spirit in our lives.

AGREEMENT

"Again, I tell you that if two of you on earth agree about anything you ask for, it will be done for you by my Father in heaven. For where two or three come together in my name, there am I with them." **Matthew 18:19-20**

ANOINTING

Oil represents the anointing. The anointing destroys the yoke. Anointing with oil and casting out demons work together. We need to clean our homes from any and all false worship idols. We also need to cleanse, anoint and dedicate each room in our homes to the Lord. Many standers, at the beginning or during their stand, have the Lord reveal to them things that need to be thrown away in their homes. Ask the Lord to help you clean your house of any ungodly objects or things. Tell the enemy he is not welcome in your home. Tell any demons who have been assigned to you or your family to be gone in the name of Jesus. Ask the Lord to put warrior angels around your home to protect you and your family from the evil one.

FASTING

Fasting is abstaining from food for a specific length of time. The Lord will convict you of the type of fast you need to go on. Some people will fast special types of foods, others will fast a meal or complete days. When I felt that I could not see the Lord moving in Bob's life or I felt the enemy strongly coming against me or my family. I would fast. God honors fasting. Some spirits will only come out through prayer and fasting.

After Jesus had gone indoors, his disciples asked him privately, "Why couldn't we drive it out?" He replied, "This kind can come out only by prayer." **Mark 9:28-29**

"Is not this the kind of fasting I have chosen; to loose the chains of injustice and untie the cords of the yoke, to set the oppressed free and break every yoke?" **Isaiah 58:6**

FREEDOM FROM SEXUAL BONDAGE

Often our spouses have opened doorways in their lives that need to be closed. A doorway is legal ground of sin that grants Satan legal access into your spouses life. A few example are pornography, adultery, drugs and alcohol.

Bob and I are one-flesh, so when Bob was in the far-country I would pray asking the Lord to close the doors that Bob had opened by his sinful lifestyle. I prayed that the Lord would open his spiritual eyes and ears to see the truth and the truth would set him free. I prayed that Bob would pray, canceling all ground that evil spirits had gained through his willful involvement in sin.

You can also pray that any "soul ties" your spouse has been involved in would be severed by the blood and cross of your Lord Jesus Christ. Pray that the Lord will speak to you and your spouse about any and all areas that need to be confessed, repented and forgiven.

Search me, O God, and know my heart; test me and know my anxious thoughts. See if there is any offensive way in me, and lead me in the way everlasting. **Psalm 139:23-24**

For the unbelieving husband has been sanctified through his wife, and the unbelieving wife has been sanctified through her believing husband. Otherwise your children would be unclean, but as it is, they are holy. **I Corinthians 7:14**

"Then you will know the truth, and the truth will set you free." **John 8:32**

Both you and your spouse can be set free from every bondage or sin in your life. Nothing is too hard for our Lord. Please use this book to know that you need to get additional information regarding binding different spirits and closing doorways that you or your spouse have opened.

You can find additional resources in your local Christian book store. Neil T. Anderson's books are excellent in finding freedom in Christ.

PRAISE

Praise is a very important key in spiritual warfare and one of the most powerful weapons available to us. Praise will defeat the enemy. When the enemy starts to attack you, praise the Lord. You are not praising the Lord for the bad circumstances, but that the Lord is with you in the midst of your circumstances. Then as we praise the Lord, He turns circumstances around to defeat the enemy. May we use Paul and Silas as examples to not let the enemy steal our peace, our joy, or our faith and love for the Lord, regardless of our circumstances.

About midnight Paul and Silas were praying and singing hymns to God, and the other prisoners were listening to them. Suddenly there was such a violent earthquake that the foundations of the prison were shaken. At once all the prison doors flew open, and everybody's chains came loose. The jailer woke up, and when he saw the prison doors open, he drew his sword and was about to kill himself because he thought the prisoners had escaped. But Paul shouted, "Don't harm yourself! We are all here!" The jailer called for lights, rushed in and fell trembling before Paul and Silas. He then brought them out and asked, "Sirs, what must I do to be saved?" They replied, "Believe in the Lord Jesus, and you will be saved--you and your household." **Acts 16:25-31**

What a promise for you and I to claim for our loved ones.

Praise him for his acts of power; praise him for his surpassing greatness....Let everything that has breath praise the Lord.... **Psalm 150:2,6**

Be joyful always; pray continually; give thanks in all circumstances, for this is God's will for you in Christ Jesus. **1 Thessalonians 5:16-18**

THE WORD AND OUR WITNESS

Everything we do in spiritual warfare must be based on the Word of God. Jesus defeated satan when He was tempted by saying, "It is written...it is written...it is written." Confess God's Word aloud as your affirmation. The more you know, the more you confess the Word, the more effective the victory will be.

Have you received a word from the Lord? I have received many for Bob, myself and my family over the past fourteen years. Ask the Lord to speak to you through His Word while you are in your quiet time with Him. When you receive a special scripture, write it in your Bible, put the date and who it is for next to the scripture. It will always be in alignment with God's Word, and consistent with God's character.

Then you can use your Sword of the Spirit by quoting the Word to the enemy to remind him of his defeat. You can quote the Word to the Lord thanking Him of the promises He has given you that you are standing and claiming on someone's behalf.

PRAYING SCRIPTURE

While I was waiting for Bob to come home from the far country, my Lord changed me first. He made me to become a new creature in Christ. I wanted to spend time with my Lord. I wanted to read His Word and pray. I often felt like I was saying and asking for the same things over and over again. I asked the Lord, "How should I pray?" He took me to **Matthew 6:9-15.** Read and study this section of scripture. During my stand, there were many books that used the Lord's Prayer as an outline for how to pray. Then the Lord showed me scriptures that Paul prayed for fellow Christians. Many books on prayer suggest you personalize these scriptures with your loved ones' names in them. I believe that there is more power in doing this than we will ever know. I went through the Bible and typed scriptures into prayers that were special to me. I suggest that you do that also. I know God's Word will not return void.

*"So is my word that goes out from my mouth: It will not return to me empty, but will accomplish what I desire and achieve the purpose for which I sent it." **Isaiah 55:11***

During my stand, I often personalized **I Corinthians 13:4-8** into a prayer:

Thank you Lord, that Bob and Charlyne are patient, that we are kind, that we do not envy, that we do not boast and we are not proud. We are not rude, we are not self-seeking, we do not get easily angered, and we keep no record of wrongs. We do not delight in evil but we both always rejoice with the truth. We will both always protect, trust, hope, and always persevere in each other. Love never fails. Amen.

On a Saturday morning, two years after Bob came home, he announced, "I have the outline for my next book." He started reading, "I Corinthians 13:4-8. Chapter 1 is Love is Patient, Chapter 2 is Love is Kind. What do you think?" Needless to say, I was crying and my heart was jumping. God showed me His power that day of personalizing and claiming the Word of God. I was so excited to be able to share with Bob why and how that scripture had been birthed into his spirit. **Believe in the power of prayer and the power of God's Word!**

Read **Psalm 119** and personalize verses for your family:

How can our children and loved ones keep their way pure? By living according to your word, I pray that _____ will seek you with all their heart; do not let them stray from your commands. I pray that _____ has hidden your word in their heart that they might not sin against you. Open my family's eyes that they may see wonderful things in your law. Your Word is a lamp to our loved one's feet and a light for their path. You are our refuge and our shield; we have put our hope in your word. Amen (Scriptures taken from: **Psalm 119:9-11,18, 105, 114)**

DON'T GIVE UP

The Lord is not slow in keeping his promise, as some understand slowness. He is patient with you, not wanting anyone to perish, but everyone to come to repentance.
2 Peter 3:9

Let us not become weary in doing good, for at the proper time we will reap a harvest if we do not give up. *Galatians 6:9*

THE LORD CAN DELIVER

*Can plunder be taken from warriors, or captives rescued from the fierce? But this is what the Lord says: "Yes, captives will be taken from warriors, and plunder retrieved from the fierce; I will contend with those who contend with you, and your children I will save." **Isaiah 49:24-25***

I wish I could come to your home and pray with you. I wish that I could sit down for two or three hours and share from my heart all that the Lord has taught me these last fourteen years. I can only try to encourage you that you CAN stand up against the enemy and say, "Enough is enough! You cannot have my husband/wife any longer! You cannot have my children any longer! Satan, you are defeated. I demand you and all your demons leave me and my family alone! Jesus Christ paid the price by shedding His blood on the cross and defeating you. I claim and stand on the promises of my Savior and Lord of my life. Greater is He that is in me than he who is in the world." Remember that your Lord is going after your lost sheep. He is calling that prodigal you love so much to come home!

*"I, the Lord, have called you in righteousness; I will take hold of your hand. I will keep you and will make you to be a covenant for the people and a light for the Gentiles, **to open eyes that are blind, to free captives from prison and to release from the dungeon those who sit in darkness." Isaiah 42:6-7** (Emphasis added)*

*I will search for the lost and bring back the strays. I will bind up the injured and strengthen the weak,.... **Ezekiel 34:16***

Your Lord *CAN* deliver your spouse from adultery, gambling, alcohol, drugs, pornography, abuse, and any other sin. Nothing is too hard for the Lord.

He is calling your spouse every day. Pray that our Lord will open ALL the prodigal's ears, eyes and hearts so that they can hear and see the truth. Pray that they will be obedient to the Lord's calling their name to come home to the Lord and to their families!

"Son of man, say to the house of Israel, 'This is what you are saying: "Our offenses and sins weigh us down, and we are wasting away because of them. How then can we live?"' Say to them, 'As surely as I live, declares the Sovereign Lord, I take no pleasure in the death of the wicked, but rather that they turn from their ways and live. Turn! Turn from your evil ways! Why will you die, O house of Israel?' **Ezekiel 33:10-11**

"I tell you that in the same way there more rejoicing in heaven over one sinner who repents than over ninety-nine righteous persons who do not need to repent." **Luke 15:7**

Bob and I want you to know that **"in Christ there is freedom."** Every person who has opened themselves to the sinful nature, can repent and be delivered from the bondage of sin.

It is necessary to break any generational curses that may have been passed on to us or for our generations to follow. We can close doors that have been opened because of our lack of knowledge and repent for our sins. We can be set free from our sinful nature and walk in the Spirit.

May the Lord increase your faith and give you hope and encouragement. Ask the Holy Spirit to teach you His principles and precepts, and then to apply them to your walk with the Lord. May the Lord rebuild and restore your family on the solid rock of Jesus Christ.

*But whenever anyone turns to the Lord, the veil is taken away. Now the Lord is the Spirit, and where the Spirit of the Lord is, there is **freedom**. And we, who with unveiled faces all* reflect the Lord's glory, are being transformed into his likeness with ever-increasing glory, which comes from the Lord, who is the Spirit. *2 Corinthians 3:16-18*

The Spirit of the Sovereign Lord is on me, because the Lord has anointed me to preach good news to the poor. He has sent me to bind up the brokenhearted, to proclaim **freedom** for the captives and release from darkness for the prisoners. *Isaiah 61:1*

I will walk about in **freedom**, for I have sought out your precepts. *Psalm 119:45*

"...He has sent me to proclaim **freedom** for the prisoners and recovery of sight for the blind, to release the oppressed, to proclaim the year of the Lord's favor." *Luke 4:18-19*

In him and through faith in him we may approach God with **freedom** and confidence. *Ephesians 3:12*

(Emphasis added)

OTHER SCRIPTURES TO HELP YOU

"If you do what is right, will you not be accepted? But if you do not do what is right, sin is crouching at your door, it desires to have you, but you must master it." **Genesis 4:7**

From the Lord comes deliverance. May your blessing be on your people. Selah **Psalm 3:8**

My eyes are ever on the Lord, for only he will release my feet from the snare. **Psalm 25:15**

Help us, O God our Savior, for the glory of your name; deliver us and forgive our sins for your name's sake. **Psalm 79:9**

Restore us, O God Almighty; make your face shine upon us, that we may be saved. **Psalm 80:7**

I seek you with all my heart; do not let me stray from your commands. I have hidden your word in my heart that I might not sin against you. **Psalm 119:10-11**

The fear of the Lord is the beginning of knowledge... **Proverbs 1:7**

Do not be afraid, for I am with you; I will bring your children from the east and gather you from the west. I will say to the north, 'Give them up!' and to the south, 'Do not hold them back.' Bring my sons from afar and my daughters from the ends of the earth--everyone who is called by my name, whom I created for my glory, whom I formed and made. **Lead out those who have eyes but are blind, who have ears but are deaf. Isaiah 43:5-8** (Emphasis added)

"I, even I, am he who blots out your transgressions, for my own sake, and remembers your sins no more." **Isaiah 43:25**

For I will pour water on the thirsty land, and streams on the dry ground; I will pour out my Spirit on your offspring, and my blessing on your descendants. They will spring up lake grass in a meadow, like poplar trees by flowing streams. One will say, 'I belong to the Lord; and other will call himself by the name of Jacob; still another will write on his hand, 'The Lord's,' and will take the name Israel. **Isaiah 44:3-5**

...To open doors before him so that gates will not be shut: I will go before you and will level the mountains; I will break down gates of bronze and cut through bars of iron. I will give you the treasures of darkness, riches stored in secret places, so that you may know that I am the Lord, the God of Israel, who summons you by name. **Isaiah 45:1-3**

Who among you fears the Lord and obeys the word of his servant? Let him who walks in the dark, who has no light, trust in the name of the Lord and rely on his God. **Isaiah 50:10**

For your Maker is your husband--the Lord Almighty is his name--the Holy One of Israel is your Redeemer; he is called the God of all the earth. The Lord will call you back as if you were a wife deserted and distressed in spirit--a wife who married young, only to be rejected," says your God. "For a brief moment I abandoned you, but with deep compassion I will bring you back." **Isaiah 54:5-7**

Call to me and I will answer you and tell you great and unsearchable things you do not know. **Jeremiah 33:3**

...They will know that I am the Lord when I break the bars of their yoke and rescue them from the hands of those who enslaved them. They will no longer be plundered by the nations, nor will wild animals devour them. They will live in safety, and no one will make them afraid. **Ezekiel 34:27-28**

" 'For I will take you out of the nations; I will gather you from all the countries and bring you back into your own land.

I will sprinkle clean water on you, and you will be clean; I will cleanse; you from all your impurities and from all your idols. I will give you a new heart and put a new spirit in you; I will remove from you your heart of stone and give you a heart of flesh. And I will put my Spirit in you and move you to follow my decrees and be careful to keep my laws. **Ezekiel 36:24-27**

Then you will remember your evil ways and wicked deeds, and you will loathe yourselves for your sins and detestable practices. I want you to know that I am not doing this for your sake, declares the Sovereign Lord. Be ashamed and disgraced for your conduct, O house of Israel! **Ezekiel 36:31-32**

" 'This is what the Sovereign Lords says: On the day I cleanse you from all your sins, I will resettle your towns, and the ruins will be rebuilt. The desolate land will be cultivated instead of lying desolate in the sight of all who pass through it. They will say, "This land that was laid waste has become like the garden of Eden, the cities that were lying in ruins, desolate and destroyed are now fortified and inhabited. Then the nations around you that remain will know that I the Lord have rebuilt what was destroyed and have replanted what was desolate. I the Lord have spoken, and I will do it.' " **Ezekiel 36:33-36**

They will no longer defile themselves with their idols and vile images or with any of their offenses, for I will save them from all their sinful backsliding, and I will cleanse them. They will be my people, and I will be their God. **Ezekiel 37:23**

"I will heal their waywardness and love them freely, for my anger has turned away from them." **Hosea 14:4**

And lead us not into temptation, but deliver us from the evil one. **Matthew 6:13**

.... "With man this impossible, but not with God; all things are possible with God." **Mark 10:27**

And these signs will accompany those who believe: In my name they will drive out demons; they will speak in new tongues;...they will place their hands on sick people, and they will get well. **Mark 16:17-18**

For we know that our old self was crucified with him so that the body of sin might be done away with, that we should no longer be slaves to sin--because anyone who has died has been freed from sin. **Romans 6:6-7**

Those who live according to the sinful nature have their minds set on what that nature desires, but those who live in accordance with the Spirit have their minds set on what the Spirit desires....Those controlled by the sinful nature cannot please God. **Romans 8:5,8**

For, "Everyone who calls on the name of the Lord will be saved." **Romans 10:13**

Do not conform any longer to the pattern of this world, but be transformed by the renewing of your mind.... **Romans 12:2**

The night is nearly over; the day is almost here. So let us put aside the deeds of darkness and put on the armor of light. Let us behave decently, as in the daytime, not in orgies and drunkenness, not in sexual immorality and debauchery, not in dissension and jealousy. Rather, clothe yourselves with the Lord Jesus Christ, and do not think about how to gratify the desires of the sinful nature. **Romans 13:12-14**

But whenever anyone turns to the Lord, the veil is taken away. Now the Lord is the Spirit, and where the Spirit of the Lord is, there is freedom. And we, who with unveiled faces all reflect the Lord's glory, are being transformed into his likeness with ever-increasing glory, which comes from the Lord, who is the Spirit. **2 Corinthians 3:16-18**

For God, who said, "Let light shine out of darkness,"

made his light shine in our hearts to give us the light of the knowledge of the glory of God in the face of Christ.
2 Corinthians 4:6

But we have this treasure in jars of clay to show that this all-surpassing power is from God and not from us. We are hard pressed on every side, but not crushed; perplexed, but not in despair; persecuted, but not abandoned; struck down, but not destroyed. **2 Corinthians 4:7-9**

Therefore we do not lose heart. Though outwardly we are wasting away, yet inwardly we are being renewed day by day. For our light and momentary troubles are achieving for us an eternal glory that far outweighs them all. So we fix our eyes not on what is seen, but on what is unseen. For what is seen is temporary, but what is unseen is eternal. **2 Corinthians 4:16-18**

We live by faith, not by sight...So we make it our goal to please him, whether we are at home in the body or away from it. **2 Corinthians 5:7**

For we must all appear before the judgment seat of Christ, that each one may receive what is due him for the things done while in the body, whether good or bad. **2 Corinthians 5:9-10**

Therefore, if anyone is in Christ, he is a new creation; the old has gone, the new has come! All this is from God, who reconciled us to himself through Christ and gave us the ministry of reconciliation: that God was reconciling the world to himself in Christ, not counting men's sins against them. And he has committed to us the message of reconciliation.
2 Corinthians 5:17-19

We are therefore Christ's ambassadors, as though God were making his appeal through us. We implore you on Christ's behalf: Be reconciled to God. God made him who had no sin to be sin for us, so that in him we might become the righteousness of God. **2 Corinthians 5:20-21**

Since we have these promises, dear friends, let us purify ourselves from everything that contaminates body and spirit, perfecting holiness out of reverence for God. **2 Corinthians 7:1**

...But because your sorrow led you to repentance. For you became sorrowful as God intended and so were not harmed in any way by us. Godly sorrow brings repentance that leads to salvation and leaves no regret, but worldly sorrow brings death. **2 Corinthians 7:9-10**

Do not be deceived: God can not be mocked. A man reaps what he sows. The one who sows to please his sinful nature, from that nature will reap destruction; the one who sows to please the Spirit, from the Spirit will reaps eternal life. Let us not become weary in doing good, for at the proper time we will reap a harvest if we do not give up. **Galatians 6:7-9**

You were taught with regard to your former way of life, to put off your old self, which is being corrupted by its deceitful desires; to be made new in the attitude of your minds; and to put on the new self, created to be like God in true righteousness and holiness. **Ephesians 4:22-24**

Nevertheless, God's solid foundation stands firm, sealed with this inscription: "The Lord knows those who are his," and, "Everyone who confesses the name of the Lord must turn away from wickedness. **2 Timothy 2:19**

Flee the evil desires of youth, and pursue righteousness, faith, love and peace, along with those who call on the Lord out of a pure heart. Don't have anything, to do with foolish and stupid arguments, because you know they produce quarrels. And the Lord's servant must not quarrel; instead, he must be kind to everyone, able to teach, not resentful. Those who oppose him he must gently instruct, in the hope that God will grant them repentance leading them to a knowledge of the truth, and that they will come to their senses and escape from the trap of the devil, who has taken them captive to do his will.

-151-

2 Timothy 2:22-26

...And how from infancy you have known the holy Scriptures, which are able to make you wise for salvation through faith in Christ Jesus. All Scripture is God-breathed and is useful for teaching, rebuking, correcting, and training in righteousness, so that the man of God may be thoroughly equipped for every good work. **2 Timothy 3:15-17**

When tempted, no one should say, "God is tempting me." For God cannot be tempted by evil, nor does he tempt anyone; but each one is tempted when, by his own evil desire, he is dragged away and enticed. Then, after desire has conceived, it gives birth to sin; and sin, when it is full-grown, gives birth to death. **James 1:13-15**

Therefore, get rid of all moral filth and the evil that is so prevalent and humbly accept the word planted in you, which can save you. **James 1:21**

Submit yourselves, then, to God. Resist the devil, and he will flee from you. Come near to God and he will come near to you. Wash your hands, you sinners, and purify your hearts, you double-minded. **James 4:7-8**

Therefore confess your sins to each other and pray for each other so that you may be healed. The prayer of a righteous man is powerful and effective. **James 5:16**

My brothers, if one of you should wander from the truth and someone should bring him back, remember this: Whoever turns a sinner from the error of his way will save him from death and cover over a multitude of sins. **James 5:19-20**

As obedient children, do not conform to the evil desires you had when you lived in ignorance. But just as he who called you is holy, so be holy in all you do: for it is written: "Be holy, because I am holy." **I Peter 1:14-16**

My dear children, I write this to you so that you will not sin. But if anybody does sin, we have one who speaks to the Father in our defense--Jesus Christ, the Righteous One. **I John 2:1**

You, dear children, are from God and have overcome them, because the one who is in you is greater than the one who is in the world. **I John 4:4**

We know that anyone born of God does not continue to sin; the one who as born of God keeps him safe, and the evil one cannot harm him. **I John 5:18**

Here I am! I stand at the door and knock. If anyone hears my voice and opens the door, I will come in and eat with him, and he with me. **Revelation 3:20**

STANDING AND PRAYING

Recently we invited visitors to the Internet site of Rejoice Ministries to share a prayer for their prodigal spouse. The few anonymous petitions shared here represent the hearts cry of scores of men and women who are asking God for freedom for their covenant mate:

"Dear Heavenly Father, speak to our prodigals and their 'others' today. Show them that the freedom they are looking for is not in doing what their flesh tells them to do, but is the freedom that You give that sets them free indeed. If need be, let them taste their freedom in their pigpens to show them how false a freedom without You is. Show them that kind of freedom is only a more restricting bondage than they have ever experienced. Then send Your Holy Spirit down to show them the true freedom that Your grace and mercy gives them so abundantly. I ask this in Jesus' sweet name. Amen."

"Father, I come before you in the name of Jesus to ask that You come to all prodigals who are running to what they think is freedom from their covenant mates. Make them see that the only true freedom comes from serving and obeying Your will for their marriage. Make their run to freedom like the pigpen of the original prodigal, so that they will see that they had it better when they were at home with their covenant mates. Break all bondage that satan has put upon our prodigals and set them free to serve You as their only true Master. I praise You that complete restoration is on its way to us standers. May you change us to be the people and spouses that You want us to be. In Jesus' name I pray."

"Lord, thank You for meeting all of our needs while our spouses are in the far country. Please bring them to salvation quickly. Let our children see Your work in their lives and want to surround themselves with good Christian friends; all for your glory, God."

"Lord, thank You for giving me the peace that surpasses all understanding. Let my light shine that my children and wife may see the blessing You give me daily."

"Lord, You are an awesome and powerful God. I pray that Your hand of healing will be upon our marriages. With the authority given me in Jesus, I move back the darkness and pray for light and truth to shine upon our prodigal spouses."

"Heal the pain and rejection, the bitterness and the turmoil, Father. I know that You are the miracle working God, and in the name of Jesus, I ask that You bring reconciliation in our families. Lord, send our spouses home. Bring them out of captivity. Where there is no love, Father give them love. Where there is no hope, give them hope. Restore us Lord, hear our cry today. Forgive us for sinning and heal our marriages, our homes, our lives, and our children's lives. Father, we do not want to leave the next generation with the curse of divorce. Please bring restoration in the name of Jesus I pray. Amen."

"Dear Lord, You know our hearts, the sadness and confusion at times is overwhelming. Clear my thoughts to see what you would have me do. Allow me to see this as part of Your plan. Guide me and my fellow standers in Your will, Amen."

"O Father, how we wait for the day, when You set our prisoners free from satan's grasp. Thank You, Dear God, for You are our hope. Our faith and trust lies with You, not in ourselves. For without You, we are nothing. Praise be to Your Holy Name. Thy will be done. Amen."

"Mighty Lord Jesus, open the hearts of our lost spouses, and let them see the evil that satan has led them to believe. Lead them home to us, and to You. Keep our children safe in Your arms, and prepare all of us for the feast of their returning. Amen."

"Father, release Your Holy Spirit to hover over our spouses and set their feet on the path of righteousness. In Jesus' name, Amen."

"Lord, I pray that You would impart a willing heart to our prodigals and that You would destroy the strongholds in their lives that have them bound to doing the will of the enemy. Satan, you are a liar and the blood of Jesus is against you!"

"Thank you Heavenly Father for being with me through these rough times. Without You in my life, it would have been too much for me to handle. I pray that You will guide me to be the mother to my daughter that I need to be. I pray for my children's salvation as well as my spouse's salvation."

"Thank You that Your ear is especially tuned to those who cry out to You. Father, I speak mercy over our prodigals for they are POW's and in need of clear vision from You. Reach their hearts by the wooing of your Holy Spirit, so that they may be restored to You in fellowship, and then restored to their families who need them so much. Thank you Father, for all of Your mercies toward us who are standing in our covenants with you."

"Father, we lift all prodigals before You. Father, we ask the Holy Spirit to minister to their hearts and turn their hearts toward home."

"Father, I take my authority in Jesus' name, and I speak purity, virtue, honor, integrity, valor, truth, and a heart of flesh into my one-flesh husband. I thank You Father, that my beloved husband walks not in the counsel of the ungodly, nor does he stand in the paths of sinners, nor does he sit in the seat of the scornful."

"My beloved husband's delight is in the law of the Lord and in God's law, my beloved husband meditates day and night. I confess that my beloved husband is like a tree, planted by the

rivers of water, that brings forth his fruit in his season,"

"Dearest Father God, please help us take back what the enemy has taken from us. Heal our hearts and touch the hearts of our prodigals with Your almighty hand. Father, change the hearts that have been turned away from you, prick them to rid them of all the impurities that satan has hardened them with, and fill them up Lord. Holy Spirit, come to them and convict them with an overwhelming desire to turn from their ways"

"Forgive us Father, when we fail You, so much of the time and cleanse us of all unrighteousness, that we will not be separated from You!! Let nothing stand in our way of having such an intimate relationship that any of our prayers be hindered!! We thank You again, Father. We worship only You, for you are worthy Father of praise."

"Lord save us all from Job's comforters. Help us also, Lord, to hold our tongues where our children are concerned. Help us to be good mothers as well as wives. Lead us in the way that we should go where our precious children are concerned. Thank you for blessing us with them."

"Father, I thank you for being here today with me and for being there with my spouse and over there with all the other standers and prodigals. Thank you for showing Your love to us over and over, for making it possible to come to you with these earthly concerns of relationships and finances. You delight in making your children happy by providing gifts, shelter, and protection. I praise you, Lord, for being all I need, yet in delighting in restoring and reconciling families. Oh, God, work on me."

"By the authority and power of the blood that Jesus shed, I rebuke and bind every demon and evil spirit that attempts to hinder any prayer request. All that come here, I ask that God protect from all evil."

"Dear Heavenly Father, please pour Your merciful blessings upon all who read these words. Speak to all prodigals to turn from their wicked ways and return home to be the Godly people that You want them to be. Change the standers in the ways that You desire, too, Lord, so that when the prodigals return, these homes will honor You."

"I pray that today all foreign relationships, addictions and habits will be broken in Your name."

"Satan, I give you your eviction papers! You get away from our spouses and our children."

"May God bless each of you today and may He send out His angels to watch over and protect us and our family members as we go to and from our places of worship."

"Satan, through the blood of Jesus, we rebuke you. Anything that you are doing that is causing marriages represented here to be destroyed, we command that you flee to the pit! You have no authority here! Leave our families alone! As for us and our houses, we will serve the Lord."

"Dear Lord, we raise that one in financial need up to You. Please arrange for the payment of the bills. We know that You can work in supernatural ways and we thank you for that."

"Lord, today we want to renew our wedding vows to you. We want to love you with all our heart, mind and soul. Lord, fill us with the joy that You want all of Your children to have. Lord, we love You and we praise You."

MY THOUGHTS ON FREEDOM

I will walk about in freedom,
for I have sought out your precepts. Psalm 119:45

MY THOUGHTS ON FREEDOM

I will walk about in freedom,
for I have sought out your precepts. Psalm 119:45

INTRODUCING

REJOICE MARRIAGE MINISTRIES

"SHARING GOOD NEWS FOR EVERY MARRIAGE"

What Is The Problem?

ONE MAN AND ONE WOMAN FOR A LIFETIME is God's perfect plan for marriage given to us in the Bible. The divorce rate in the United States is above 50 percent. Men and women who once stood at an altar before God and pledged to each other "for better, for worse, for richer, for poorer, in sickness and in health, to love and to cherish, *till death do us part*" are leaving home to pursue selfish desires. They become prodigals, leaving behind brokenhearted children and wounded spouses. Many go on to other marriages, the large percentage of which also fail. Divorce is also attacking families within the church. Satan is out to steal, kill, and destroy families and marriages.

What Is The Provision?

There is a solution to the divorce problem. Our Lord Jesus Christ can heal hurting marriages, even when only one of those involved turns to Christ, seeking marriage restoration. *REJOICE MINISTRIES* was born out of the needs of hurting couples. All across our nation are thousands of spouses who are standing and praying for God to restore their marriages. We invite you to allow us to stand and pray with you for the restoration of your marriage and home, regardless of circumstances.

THE STEINKAMPS

We were divorced after 19 years of marriage. Our three children became victims of a broken home as Bob became a prodigal spouse and left for the far country. Neither of us realized that satan desires to break up families and destroy marriages.

Charlyne searched the scriptures and discovered that God hates divorce. She found that our Lord Jesus Christ restores and rebuilds marriages, when a mate will love the prodigal unconditionally, as Christ loves us. Charlyne committed herself to a sacrificial stand for the restoration of our marriage. To the glory of God, we were remarried to each other on July 7, 1987.

Today, God allows our family to minister His love, forgiveness, and restoration to others with broken marriages. A newsletter is distributed nationwide. An army of prayer partners, pray daily by name for those with hurting marriages. We also maintain a 24-Hour Encouragement Line for spouses standing for God's restoration of their marriages. We desire to be an encouragement as you stand for the healing of your marriage.

"But blessed is the man who trusts in the Lord, whose confidence is in him." Jeremiah 17:7

DO YOU REALLY WANT

A

DIVORCE?

There Is Help Available

- Books and tapes to encourage you.

- Bible study material to help you learn and grow in God's word

- Newsletters

- Prayer partners to stand and agree with you in prayer

- Testimonies of others with restored marriages.

"Be strong and courageous. Do not be afraid or terrified...for the Lord your God goes with you; he will never leave you nor forsake you." Deuteronomy 31:6

REJOICE MARRIAGE MINISTRIES
Bob and Charlyne Steinkamp
P.O. Box 11242
Pompano Beach, Florida 33061
(954) 941-6508
FAX (954) 781-7076

www.stopdivorce.org

ADDITIONAL MATERIAL
AVAILABLE FROM
REJOICE MARRIAGE MINISTRIES

BOOKS BY THE STEINKAMPS
* "Prodigals Do Come Home"
* "The Twelve Days of....?"
* "Thoughts On Restoring a Marriage"
* "After The Prodigal Returns/
    Standing After The Prodigal Returns"
* "More Thoughts On Restoring A Marriage"
* "Chicagoman"
* "Good News OnLine"
* "Charlyne Cares"
* "Be Healed"

SELECTED CASSETTE TAPES
* The Steinkamp's Testimony
* Potential Prodigal
* *Unshackled!* Radio Testimony
* Prayer (Set of three tapes)
* He Set the Captives Free
* Are You Willing To Pay The Price?
* Study in Ephesians (Set of seven tapes)
* Standing For God's Best
* The Sovereignty of God
* Don't Give Up!
* Spiritual Warfare Series -*NEW*- (Set of three tapes)

Many of the teachings at our weekly Rejoice Bible study have been taped. Please contact us for an updated list of over fifty tapes that are available.

YOUR RESPONSE

REJOICE MARRIAGE MINISTRIES
P.O. Box 11242
Pompano Beach, Florida 33061

____Please add me to the newsletter mailing list.

____Please send information on marriage restoration.

____I want to help.

Enclosed is my donation $ _____ (tax deductible)

(Please Print Plainly)

_____
NAME

_____
ADDRESS

_____
CITY, STATE, ZIP CODE

_____
PHONE   E-MAIL

_____
MY SPOUSE'S NAME

_____
MY PRAYER REQUEST

_____

_____

THE GREATEST NEWS

That if you confess with your mouth, " Jesus is Lord," and believe in your heart that God raised him from the dead, you will be saved. Romans 10:9

Many have found the first step in a healed marriage is to have a personal relationship with Jesus Christ. Our God and Creator is waiting to hear your prayer. Have you received Jesus Christ as Lord and Savior of your life? He will save you and be your Comforter and Counselor in the days ahead, regardless of the circumstances.

A Prayer For You

Dear Jesus, I believe that You died for me and that You rose again on the third day. I confess to you that I am a sinner and that I need Your love and forgiveness. Come into my life, forgive me for my sins, and give me eternal life. I confess to you now that You are my Lord and Savior. Thank You for my salvation. Lord, show me Your will and your way for my marriage. Mold me and make me to be the spouse I need to be for my spouse. Thank you for rebuilding my marriage. Amen.

Signed_____

Date_____

"Believe in the Lord Jesus, and you will be saved--you and your household." Acts 16:31

MY THOUGHTS ON FREEDOM

I will walk about in freedom,
for I have sought out your precepts. Psalm 119:45

MY THOUGHTS ON FREEDOM

I will walk about in freedom,
for I have sought out your precepts. Psalm 119:45